Letters and Papers from Prison

by Dietrich Bonhoeffer

Dietrich Bonhoeffer

Letters and Papers from Prison

REVISED EDITION

Edited by Eberhard Bethge

New York: The Macmillan Company

Library of Congress Catalog Card Number: 67–19951
First published in English 1953
New Edition, Revised and Enlarged, 1967

(Originally published as *Prisoner for God*)

THE MACMILLAN COMPANY, NEW YORK

Printed in the United States of America

Translated from the German
Widerstand und Ergebung
Briefe und Aufzeichnungen aus der Haft
(Chr. Kaiser Verlag, München, 12th edition, 1964)
by Reginald Fuller
and revised by Frank Clarke and others

CONTENTS

v

ILLUSTRATIONS

(between pages 104–105)

EDITOR'S FOREWORD

IT WAS NOT till five years after 1945 that I overcame my reluctance to take out of my desk the letters and papers that Dietrich Bonhoeffer had written in prison, and submit extracts from them, in the form of a small volume, to friends and others who might be interested. I scarcely dared to hope that my effort on behalf of his "incomplete ideas," as he himself called them (p. 88), could stand the critical test of a wider publicity.

Then came the first word of encouragement, from Gerhard Ebeling. He expressed the opinion that the volume was "essentially a kind of anthology"; he found in the wealth of its contents "a surprising confirmation of the idea that I am a pupil of Bonhoeffer, even in questions where I progressed beyond the time of Finkenwalde, and which have taken me along a way that, as I now realize, was his way too" (30.9.1951).

The next answer came from Helmut Thielicke: "*Letters and Papers from Prison* completely filled last week; it exercised on me an intensity and living power such as I had not felt for years" (11.10.1951).

The third response was Ronald Gregor Smith's decision to have the book translated into English at once.

Now, fifteen years have passed, during which *Letters and Papers from Prison* has made its way across the world. It has encouraged people and perplexed them. It has made them uneasy and compelled them to draw radical conclusions. It has introduced into the debate formulas which at first seemed puzzling but suddenly became current coin.

So far, no unanimous opinion has developed as to what is the essence of the man and his message. Why is he so important—what is there about him? Is it the theologian, or is it the martyr? Some critics put an "only" before the designation that they prefer. Is he only an orthodox person dressed as a liberal, or is he a modernist? Are we to judge him by his monastic experiments, or by his resolve to become a conspirator? Is he to be ranged with Karl Barth, or with Rudolf Bultmann? Does his theology belong to systematic theology, or to ethics? Is its secret to be found in ecclesiology, or in Christology? Can we, indeed, attach this visionary to any logical system? All this is being asked. It seems to me, however, that a clear-cut answer to any of these questions is achieved at the cost of throwing the picture as a whole out of balance. A clear-cut answer is always something more or something less. Does not the secret of this book consist in its actually uniting these alternatives? Interest in an ordinary best-seller flares up suddenly, and then dies down just as fast; but this book invites us to return to it years later, when we have tried for ourselves to take the ways that it suggests.

In the discussion of Bonhoeffer's last fragmentary writings, the emphasis has varied greatly. In Germany, interest centred on questions of hermeneutics, the theological theory of knowledge; and there it remained almost exclusively for a long time. In England, on the other hand, much more stress was at once laid on the question of the consequences for ecclesiology and on the form of a "worldly" devotional life. In America, students seem to decide that, according to Bonhoeffer, the first and only problems to be solved are those of ethics—one must therefore demonstrate for civil rights

—before any devotional commitments are again undertaken.

Thus in the German-speaking and the English-speaking areas respectively a different use of important technical terms came to be adopted. The Germans always speak for a "non-religious *interpretation*," whereas the English-speaking peoples prefer a "non-religious *Christianity*." Bonhoeffer himself nearly always uses "non-religious interpretation." He only once uses "non-religious Christianity" (to be more exact, "religionless") —but it does occur. Behind this difference of stress, which is not very much noticed, there is in each case a different chain of tradition.

German theology is dominated by the concept of "proclamation" (*Verkündigung*)—a word that is difficult to translate simply and adequately into English; it has different connotations for different people. So in Germany people were mainly concerned to hear what help Bonhoeffer could provide in the task of preaching, and the questions he raised were discussed in regard to questions of understanding and problems of translation. The Bultmann debate was already in full swing when the book appeared in 1951; that debate greeted "non-religious interpretation" as a variant of "existentialist interpretation," and fitted it in accordingly. Everything seemed to be converging on "interpretation," and any ecclesiological implications and ethical elements in Bonhoeffer's work remained in the background. In fact, there are emphases in Bonhoeffer's remarks which lend support to Bultmann at the expense of Karl Barth, and there are passages that fit well into that discussion. When in 1963 the debate was unexpectedly enlivened by Dr. J. A. T. Robinson's *Honest to God*, which likewise suggested a similarity between Bonhoeffer and Bultmann, it was already well-worn; it had penetrated into the remotest clerical assemblies and been hawked round in fundamentalist parish circles. So the theological experts in Germany could find nothing to say about Dr. Robinson's book, except that it contained nothing new. Many of them restricted themselves to the early chapters, which in fact deal with problems in the theory of knowledge. They hardly got as far as the second half, where the ecclesiological and ethical questions are raised so passionately—and where, in my opinion, Dr. Robinson is nearer to Bonhoeffer than in the first part.

The English public approached these fragmentary writings by Bonhoeffer much more directly, asking what hierarchy, community, liturgy, and devotional life—and ethical decisions—might signify for a "non-religious Christianity," and how they were to be renewed or fashioned in a non-religious way. "Religionless Christianity" therefore at once appeared to some as something much more absurd, and to others as something incomparably more radical, than it did in Germany. In Germany indeed, under Gerhard Ebeling's guidance, it had been disputed whether Bonhoeffer's programme meant that questions might at once be raised about the Church's form, and so the real problem of how to present the gospel afresh in a non-religious way was concealed. Now it can hardly be doubted that Bonhoeffer's whole life and work are characterized throughout by personal involvement, in an attempt to provide answers in the realm of daily life, and that, in *Letters and Papers from Prison*, questions of the theory of knowledge and hermeneutics go hand in glove with the question of the form that is actually brought into being. Bonhoeffer is wholly concerned to see these questions all along, not as two questions, but as a unity, and he is concerned to start from that unity and to move towards it. Is not his secret just here, that his theology, ecclesiology, and ethics have become so interdependent, in fact interchangeable? So far, the justification of the

English emphasis in the debate is in Bonhoeffer himself. But perhaps one may ask whether the English point of view does not press on too early and too quickly to the possibilities of realizing these new insights. Practical verification in church constitution and ideals of piety are made the criteria, criteria in a situation where great perseverance is needed before the new insights (which are by nature opposed to what we had in practice been used to) can produce their own new forms. Must we not resist the question whether and how the gospel is rightly and adequately to be kept present—i.e. "interpreted?"

One contribution that the English linguistic usage can make to the German discussion is a reminder that one cannot argue for decades about "questions of interpretation" without tackling questions of form. These have recently been raised more insistently in the *Kirchentag*, and are calling up a new wave of protest and suspicion. In the English discussion, is it not even clearer that ecclesiology and ethics live only from the mystery of Christology, and are both judged and refashioned by it?

It is the unity (not the unification) of the three elements—theology, ecclesiology, and ethics—that so attracts one to Bonhoeffer. He can hardly fail to disquiet anyone who yields to the temptation to resolve the tension of these elements in favour of any one of them. He was willing to take such risks for civil rights as to engage in conspiracy, and yet he did not simply leave behind him the devotional practice of a long life. He sharply criticized his church's centuries-old privileges and demand for security, its anxiety about material things, its hierarchical pattern and its juridically constructed doctrines; he broke down its traditional boundary-posts—and yet he loved his earthly church to the end. He learnedly analysed the different trends of theological history so as not to slur over any difficulties—

and yet he made every effort to simplify as much and as convincingly as possible.

A Roman Catholic who was reading Bonhoeffer's *Letters and Papers from Prison* told me that, whereas all the rumpus had led her to expect a shockingly destructive work, she was increasingly surprised, as she read page after page of the original, how different it all was; it did not begin with any aggressive or heretical themes, and there was no mention of "religionless Christianity" in the first hundred pages and more. The dominating impression left on her was not that of the words of praise or blame that had been bandied round, but of a world of genuine unforced piety. She felt that everything that Bonhoeffer had said in his critical and tentative way was in fact founded on devotion and trusting optimism.

Fifteen years ago we were moved to go on by the newly formulated doctrines that we found in Bonhoeffer's work—admittedly only in the brief last third of the book, and there, in fact, accompanied by his question about the place of devotion in a "secret discipline." Now the hearers are surprised at discovering here the formulas that have since become current. The woman in question felt attracted to go on to investigate what she had hitherto supposed to be unprofitable. A reading of the original source convinced her that it was not a matter of moderate dilutions, but of a deeper present encounter with God, here and now, in Jesus of Nazareth.

Bonhoeffer's simplified description of Jesus as "the man for others" does indeed show an insight gained only through prolonged effort. It means the realization of the fundamental difference between the religious God who is all-powerful, and the Christian God who suffers and is powerless; between the image of a religious God who keeps mankind in despotic tutelage, and that of a Christian God who exposes and judges men's craving for power. It means the realization of the difference between religious institutions that keep men from growing up to think and decide for themselves, and a society that resolves in love and freedom all desire to exert, or to live under, forcible control. It means the realization of the difference between going forward together and suffering together.

This Roman Catholic had not supposed that so much was involved, or that one's outlook on the world, one's intellect, ethics, and trials were so interwoven. A Jew wrote to me, after reading *Letters and Papers from Prison*, that he was beginning to see for the first time why Jesus could be regarded as divine. For all its fragmentary nature, the book lives because it brings to birth again, in our own generation, the joy of discovering the Christian nature of Christianity.

EDITOR'S PREFACE

DIETRICH BONHOEFFER'S FATHER was a distinguished doctor and psychiatrist, who taught at Berlin University; and his forebears included mayors and clergymen. In the church of Schwäbisch-Hall, Württemberg, there are old tombstones with the name Bonhoeffer. Dietrich's mother was a granddaughter of Karl von Hase, who was Professor of Church History in Jena, and who was also imprisoned for a time because of his zeal for the freedom of students' associations.

Dietrich, who was one of a large family,[1] was born in Breslau on 4 February 1906. In Grunewald, Berlin, he played with the children of Adolf von Harnack the theologian, and of Hans Delbrück the historian. In the summer of 1924 he became a student of theology at Berlin University, where he took his first degree as *Lizentiat* three years later with a thesis on *Communio Sanctorum*. Although Harnack, Seeberg, and Lietzmann, three of the most influential teachers in Berlin, thought highly of him, he came more and more under

[1] Karl-Friedrich (1899–1957), Professor of Natural Science, married to Grete von Dohnanyi; Walter (1899–1918), killed in the First World War; Klaus (1901–45), a lawyer, married to Emmi Delbrück; Ursula (born 1902, married to Professor Rüdiger Schleicher (killed 1945); Christine (1903–65), married to Dr. Hans von Dohnanyi (killed 1945); Dietrich (1906–45); Sabine (born 1906), married to Professor Gerhard Leibholz; Susanne (born 1909), married to Professor Walter Dress.

the influence of Karl Barth, whom he had not yet heard lecture. This influence can be seen in his later University thesis, *Akt und Sein*, in which he acknowledges the importance of dialectical theology for the history of philosophy and theology.

After a short period as pastor in Barcelona (1928-9), and a year's study at Union Theological Seminary, New York (1930), he began to teach in the theological faculty of Berlin University, where he continued, with some intervals, till 1936, when he was forbidden to teach by the Nazi authorities. The most important break during those years was when he became pastor of two German congregations in London, the Reformed Church of St. Paul and the German Evangelical Church in Sydenham, from 1933-5. His reason for this step was his wish to make an unequivocal protest against the submission of the "German Christians" in Germany to Hitler's totalitarian régime. From this time he became one of the leading interpreters of German events for the western churches.

While he was preparing, jointly with C. F. Andrews, for a visit to Gandhi, he received a call from the "Confessing Church" in Germany (which opposed the Nazi-sponsored "German Christian" Church movement) to return home in order to lead an emergency seminary in Pomerania for young ministers. It was in this task that Bonhoeffer's personal and theological influence was at its greatest. Here he wrote two books rejecting compromise in the Church struggle, *The Cost of Discipleship* (*Die Nachfolge*, 1937) and *Life Together* (*Gemeinsames Leben*, 1938)—the two works that did most during his lifetime to make his name and his thoughts widely known.

While the discussion of his stirring attack on "cheap grace" in *The Cost of Discipleship* was going on, developments of a quite different kind were beginning to change radically the direction of his life and thought.

Through his brother-in-law Hans von Dohnanyi he was
given a glimpse behind the scenes of the crisis that centred on General von Fritsch, and of the plans for over-
throwing the Nazi government that were associated with
General Beck. Up till then Bonhoeffer, under American
and English influences, had been very near to absolute
pacifism—a virtually unheard-of position in Germany
at that time. Now he began to see pacifism as an il-
legitimate escape, especially if it tempted him to with-
draw from his increasing contacts with the responsible
political and military leaders of the resistance to Hitler.
He no longer saw any way of escape into some region
of piety. In 1939, when he was on a lecture tour in
America, he was urgently pressed by his American
friends to stay there and take up some work that suited
his ecumenical spirit and his fine sensitivity to church
life abroad; but he decided to return to Germany, into
what was obviously a deteriorating situation, and he
took one of the last ships to leave for Germany before
the war. While he was still in America, he wrote in his
diary: "I do not understand why I am here. . . . The
short prayer in which we thought of our German brothers almost overwhelmed me. . . . If things become more
uncertain, I shall certainly go back to Germany. . . .
If war comes, I shall not stay in America . . ." and finally, "Since I came on board ship, my mental turmoil
about the future has gone."

His life was now divided between the tasks of the
Confessing Church, visiting, working on his *Ethics*
(*Ethik*, which appeared posthumously and unfinished
in 1949), and the tasks of the Resistance movement,
with all the journeyings that they involved. Of these,
the most difficult and impressive was a visit to Stock-
holm in 1942, to have conversations with Dr. G. K. A.
Bell, the Bishop of Chichester. The Gestapo put all
kinds of obstacles in the way of his church work, for-
bidding him to lecture, write, make speeches, or remain

in Berlin; while on the other hand he was quietly provided with all the passes and papers that a privileged courier needed. Extraordinary confidence was thus placed in him; but it did not last. One morning in April 1943 we heard that Hans von Dohnanyi had been arrested in his office, and we waited for the motor-car to draw up before Bonhoeffer's door. We made the room as ready as we could for the expected visit—documents were placed in safety, and others, which might provide misleading and unimportant information, were left on the table. Things took their expected course, and Bonhoeffer was arrested.

He spent the first eighteen months of his imprisonment (from 5 April 1943 to 8 October 1944) in the military section of the prison at Tegel, Berlin. After some initial quibbling, he was allowed to write to his parents. The first part of this book consists of selections from the letters that he wrote to them. The fact that they were read by the prison censor, and in particular by the chief judicial investigator, Dr. Roeder, of course influenced their contents; but still more obvious is Bonhoeffer's concern to allay the anxieties of his family.

After six months, however, Bonhoeffer had made such good friends among the warders and medical orderlies that he was able to embark on an extensive correspondence, partly by letter and partly on scraps of paper, with various people including the present editor. But certain precautions were needed; thus, communications about certain people who might be in danger, about the progress of the resistance movement, and about the investigations into his own case, had to be made guardedly in code. But the correspondence went on till more stringent measures were taken after the unsuccessful attempt to assassinate Hitler on 20 July, and the discovery of the Zossen papers (documents, diaries, and other evidence relating to the members of the resistance movement associated with Canaris, Oster, Hans von Dohnanyi, and others) in September 1944. As a result, Bonhoeffer was removed by the Gestapo to close confinement in Prinz-Albrecht-Strasse. Unfortunately this move, together with the arrest of the editor in October 1944, meant that the last month's letters from Tegel had to be destroyed; the other letters had been put in a safe place. These letters form the second part of this volume. Here, away from prying eyes, Bonhoeffer speaks freely of experiences, thoughts, and feelings.

With these letters he enclosed some of his written work, consisting of prayers, poems, and reflections. The short account of his imprisonment (p. 81) was meant for the information of his uncle, General von Hase, who was then responsible as Commandant of Berlin.

Page by page, these letters show us a picture of life in a prison cell, as it was experienced in all its aspects, with the intimate details of an individual life fused into a striking unity with the disastrous events that were going on in the world outside, a unity produced by an outstanding mind and a sensitive heart. All this is summarized most movingly in the short letter of 21 July 1944 and in the "Stations on the road to freedom," when Bonhoeffer had learnt of the failure of 20 July and was convinced that his end was near. The failure of the plot was a terrible blow for him, but he met it with renewed dedication to the service of his people, and with steadfast determination to bear all the painful consequences. In time to come it will be better appreciated how this second act of dedication, which could and did only lead to martyrdom, justified the first, the activities which flowed from and sealed it as an indestructible heritage, which may lie dormant but can never be lost.

In Prinz-Albrecht-Strasse opportunities of contact were greatly reduced. The acceptance and dispatch of messages and the necessities of life depended entirely on the caprice of the commissars. One day Dietrich's family found out that he had disappeared; and the

Gestapo refused to give any information as to his where-abouts. That was in February. It was not till the early summer of 1945, some time after Germany's collapse, that we learnt what had happened to him. He had been removed first to Buchenwald, then to Schönberg, and finally to Flossenbürg. Now the circumstances of his end, on 9 April 1945, are gradually coming to light. The letters from prison are preceded by an essay entitled "After ten years." This was composed at the turn of the year 1942–3, and sent to a few friends as a Christmas present. At that time warnings had already been received, especially by Hans von Dohnanyi, that the Central Bureau for the Security of the Reich was collecting evidence against Bonhoeffer and was bent on his arrest. This fragmentary essay was stowed away among the beams and rafters, where it survived the attentions of the police and of enemy bombs. It is a testimony to the spirit in which we lived and suffered at the time.

Bonhoeffer's last weeks were spent with prisoners drawn from all over Europe. Among them was Payne Best, an English officer. In his book *The Venlo Incident* he writes: "Bonhoeffer . . . was all humility and sweetness; he always seemed to me to diffuse an atmosphere of happiness, of joy in every smallest event in life, and of deep gratitude for the mere fact that he was alive. . . . He was one of the very few men that I have ever met to whom God was real and close." And again: "The following day, Sunday 8th April, 1945, Pastor Bonhoeffer held a little service and spoke to us in a manner which reached the hearts of all, finding just the right words to express the spirit of our imprisonment and the thoughts and resolutions which it brought. He had hardly finished his last prayer when the door opened and two evil-looking men in civilian clothes came in and said: "Prisoner Bonhoeffer, get ready to come with us." Those words "come with us"—for all prisoners they had come to mean one thing only—the scaffold.

"We bade him good-bye—he drew me aside—'This is the end,' he said. 'For me the beginning of life,' and then he gave a message to give, if I could, to the Bishop of Chichester . . . Next day, at Flossenbürg, he was hanged."

That was in Schönberg, a little village in the Bavarian forest. A school classroom was his last halting-place, and men from every country of Europe and of differing creeds were his last companions on earth.

EBERHARD BETHGE

Acknowledgements are due to Mr. J. B. Leishman for the English version of the poem on p. 188, and to Mr. Geoffrey Winthrop Young for the poems on pp. 173, 192, and 213.

I

AFTER TEN YEARS

TEN YEARS IS a long time in anyone's life. As time is the most valuable thing that we have, because it is the most irrevocable, the thought of any lost time troubles us whenever we look back. Time lost is time in which we have failed to live a full human life, gain experience, learn, create, enjoy, and suffer; it is time that has not been filled up, but left empty. These last years have certainly not been like that. Our losses have been great and immeasurable, but time has not been lost. It is true that the knowledge and experience that were gained, and of which one did not become conscious till later, are only abstractions of reality, of life actually lived. "But just as the capacity to forget is a gift of grace, so memory, the recalling of lessons we have learnt, is also part of responsible living." In the following pages I should like to try to give some account of what we have experienced and learnt in common during these years —not personal experiences, or anything systematically arranged, or arguments and theories, but conclusions reached more or less in common by a circle of like-minded people, and related to the business of human life, put down one after the other, the only connection between them being that of concrete experience. There is nothing new about them, for they were known long before; but it has been given to us to reach them anew by first-hand experience. One cannot write about these things without a constant sense of gratitude for the fellowship of spirit and community of life that have been proved and preserved throughout these years.

No Ground under our Feet

One may ask whether there have ever before in human history been people with so little ground under their feet—people to whom every available alternative seemed equally intolerable, repugnant, and futile, who looked beyond all these existing alternatives for the source of their strength so entirely in the past or in the future, and who yet, without being dreamers, were able to await the success of their cause so quietly and confidently. Or perhaps one should rather ask whether the responsible thinking people of any generation that stood at a turning-point in history did not feel much as we do, simply because something new was emerging that could not be seen in the existing alternatives.

Who stands fast?

The great masquerade of evil has played havoc with all our ethical concepts. For evil to appear disguised as light, charity, historical necessity, or social justice is quite bewildering to anyone brought up on our traditional ethical concepts, while for the Christian who bases his life on the Bible it merely confirms the fundamental wickedness of evil.

The *reasonable* people's failure is obvious. With the best intentions and a naïve lack of realism, they think that with a little reason they can bend back into position the framework that has got out of joint. In their lack of vision they want to do justice to all sides, and so the conflicting forces wear them down with nothing achieved. Disappointed by the world's unreasonableness, they step aside in resignation or collapse before the stronger party.

Still more pitiable is the total collapse of moral *fanaticism*. The fanatic thinks that his single-minded principles qualify him to do battle with the powers of evil; but like a bull he rushes at the red cloak instead of at the person who is holding it; he exhausts himself and is beaten. He gets entangled in non-essentials and falls into the trap set by cleverer people.

Then there is the man with a *conscience*, who fights single-handed against heavy odds in situations that call for a decision. But the scale of the conflicts in which he has to choose—with no advice or support except from his own conscience—tears him to pieces. Evil approaches him in so many respectable and seductive disguises that his conscience becomes nervous and vacillating, till at last he contents himself with a salved instead of a clear conscience, so that he lies to his own conscience in order to avoid despair; for a man whose only support is his conscience can never realize that a bad conscience may be stronger and more wholesome than a deluded one.

From the perplexingly large number of possible decisions, the way of *duty* seems to be the sure way out. Here, what is commanded is accepted as what is most certain, and the responsibility for it rests on the commander, not on the person commanded. But no one who confines himself to the limits of duty ever goes so far as to venture, on his sole responsibility, to act in the only way that makes it possible to score a direct hit on evil and defeat it. The man of duty will in the end have to do his duty by the devil too.

As to the man who asserts his complete *freedom* to stand four-square to the world, who values the necessary deed more highly than an unspoilt conscience or reputation, who is ready to sacrifice a barren principle for a fruitful compromise, or the barren wisdom of a middle course for a fruitful radicalism—let him beware lest his freedom should bring him down. He will assent to what is bad so as to ward off something worse, and in doing so he will no longer be able to realize that the worse, which he wants to avoid, might be the better. Here we have the raw material of tragedy.

Here and there people flee from public altercation into the sanctuary of private *virtuousness*. But anyone who does this must shut his mouth and his eyes to the injustice around him. Only at the cost of self-deception can he keep himself pure from the contamination arising from responsible action. In spite of all that he does, what he leaves undone will rob him of his peace of mind. He will either go to pieces because of this disquiet, or become the most hypocritical of Pharisees.

Who stands fast? Only the man whose final standard is not his reason, his principles, his conscience, his freedom, or his virtue, but who is ready to sacrifice all this when he is called to obedient and responsible action in faith and in exclusive allegiance to God—the responsible man, who tries to make his whole life an answer to the question and call of God. Where are these responsible people?

Civil Courage?

What lies behind the complaint about the dearth of civil courage? In recent years we have seen a great deal of bravery and self-sacrifice, but civil courage hardly anywhere, even among ourselves. To attribute this simply to personal cowardice would be too facile a psychology; its background is quite different. In a long history, we Germans have had to learn the need for and the strength of obedience. In the subordination of all personal wishes and ideas to the tasks to which we have been called, we have seen the meaning and the greatness of our lives. We have looked upwards, not in servile fear, but in free trust, seeing in our tasks a call, and in our call a vocation. This readiness to follow a command from "above" rather than our own private opinions and wishes was a sign of legitimate self-distrust. Who would deny that in obedience, in their task and calling, the Germans have again and again shown the utmost bravery and self-sacrifice? But the German has kept his freedom—and what nation has talked more passionately of freedom than the Germans, from Luther to the idealist philosophers?—by seeking deliverance from self-will through service to the community. Calling and freedom were to him two sides of the same thing. But in this he misjudged the world; he did not realize that his submissiveness and self-sacrifice could be exploited for evil ends. When that happened, the exercise of the calling itself became questionable, and all the moral principles of the German were bound to totter. The fact could not be escaped that the German still lacked something fundamental: he could not see the need for free and responsible action, even in opposition to his task and his calling; in its place there appeared on the one hand an irresponsible lack of scruple, and on the other a self-tormenting punctiliousness that never led to action. Civil courage, in fact, can grow only out of the free responsibility of free men. Only now are the Germans beginning to discover the meaning of free responsibility. It depends on a God who demands responsible action in a bold venture of faith, and who promises forgiveness and consolation to the man who becomes a sinner in that venture.

Of Success

Although it is certainly not true that success justifies an evil deed and shady means, it is impossible to regard success as something that is ethically quite neutral. The fact is that historical success creates a basis for the continuance of life, and it is still a moot point whether it is ethically more responsible to take the field like a Don Quixote against a new age, or to admit one's defeat, accept the new age, and agree to serve it. In the last resort success makes history; and the ruler of history repeatedly brings good out of evil over the heads of the history-makers. Simply to ignore the ethical significance of success is a short-circuit created by dogmatists who think unhistorically and irresponsibly; and it is good for us sometimes to be compelled to grapple seriously with the ethical problem of success. As long as goodness is successful, we can afford the luxury of regarding it as having no ethical significance; it is when success is achieved by evil means that the problem arises. In the face of such a situation we find that it cannot be adequately dealt with, either by theoretical dogmatic arm-chair criticism, which means a refusal to face the facts, or by opportunism, which means giving up the struggle and surrendering to success. We will not and must not be either outraged critics or opportunists, but must take our share of responsibility for the moulding of history in every situation and at every moment, whether we are the victors or the vanquished. One who will not allow any occurrence whatever to deprive him of his responsibility for the course of history—because he knows that it has been laid on him by God—will thereafter achieve a more fruitful relation to the events of history than that of barren criticism and equally barren opportunism. To talk of going down fighting like heroes in the face of certain defeat is not really heroic at all, but merely a refusal to face the future. The ultimate question for a responsible man to ask is not how he is to extricate himself heroically from the affair, but how the coming generation is to live. It is only from this question, with its responsibility towards history, that fruitful solutions can come, even if for the time being they are very humiliating. In short, it is much easier to see a thing through from the point of view of abstract principle than from that of concrete responsibility. The rising generation will always instinctively discern which of these we make the basis of our actions, for it is their own future that is at stake.

Of Folly

Folly is a more dangerous enemy to the good than evil. One can protest against evil; it can be unmasked and, if need be, prevented by force. Evil always carries the seeds of its own destruction, as it makes people, at the least, uncomfortable. Against folly we have no defence. Neither protests nor force can touch it; reasoning is no use; facts that contradict personal prejudices can simply be disbelieved—indeed, the fool can counter by criticizing them, and if they are undeniable, they can just be pushed aside as trivial exceptions. So the fool, as distinct from the scoundrel, is completely self-satisfied; in fact, he can easily become dangerous, as it does not take much to make him aggressive. A fool must therefore be treated more cautiously than a scoundrel; we shall never again try to convince a fool by reason, for it is both useless and dangerous.

If we are to deal adequately with folly, we must try to understand its nature. This much is certain, that it is a moral rather than an intellectual defect. There are people who are mentally agile but foolish, and people who are mentally slow but very far from foolish—a discovery that we make to our surprise as a result of particular situations. We thus get the impression that folly is likely to be, not a congenital defect, but one that is acquired in certain circumstances where people *make* fools of themselves or allow others to make fools of them. We notice further that this defect is less common in the unsociable and solitary than in individuals or groups that are inclined or condemned to sociability. It seems, then, that folly is a sociological rather than a psychological problem, and that it is a special form of the operation of historical circumstances on people, a psychological by-product of definite external factors. If we look more closely, we see that any violent display of power, whether political or religious, produces an outburst of folly in a large part of mankind; indeed, this seems actually to be a psychological and sociological law: the power of some needs the folly of the others. It is not that certain human capacities, intellectual capacities for instance, become stunted or destroyed, but rather that the upsurge of power makes such an overwhelming impression that men are deprived of their independent judgment, and—more or less unconsciously —give up trying to assess the new state of affairs for themselves. The fact that the fool is often stubborn must not mislead us into thinking that he is independent. One feels in fact, when talking to him, that one is dealing, not with the man himself, but with slogans, catchwords, and the like, which have taken hold of him. He is under a spell, he is blinded, his very nature is being misused and exploited. Having thus become a passive instrument, the fool will be capable of any evil and at the same time incapable of seeing that it is evil. Here lies the danger of a diabolical exploitation that can do irreparable damage to human beings.

But at this point it is quite clear, too, that folly can be overcome, not by instruction, but only by an act of liberation; and so we have to come to terms with the fact that in the great majority of cases inward liberation must be preceded by outward liberation, and that until that has taken place, we may as well abandon all attempts to convince the fool. In this state of affairs we have to realize why it is no use our trying to find out what "the people" really think, and why the question is so superfluous for the man who thinks and acts responsibly—but always given these particular circumstances. The Bible's words that "the fear of the Lord is the beginning of wisdom" (Ps. 111.10) tell us that a person's inward liberation to live a responsible life before God is the only real cure for folly.

But there is some consolation in these thoughts on folly: they in no way justify our thinking that most people are fools in all circumstances. What will really matter is whether those in power expect more from people's folly than from their wisdom and independence of mind.

Contempt for Humanity?

There is a very real danger of our drifting into an attitude of contempt for humanity. We know quite well that we have no right to do so, and that it would lead us into the most sterile relation to our fellow-men. The following thoughts may keep us from such a temptation. It means that we at once fall into the worst blunders of our opponents. The man who despises another will never be able to make anything of him. Nothing that we despise in the other man is entirely absent from ourselves. We often expect from others more than we are willing to do ourselves. Why have we hitherto thought so intemperately about man and his frailty and temptability? We must learn to regard people less in the light of what they do or omit to do, and more in the light of what they suffer. The only profitable relationship to others—and especially to our weaker brethren —is one of love, and that means the will to hold fellowship with them. God himself did not despise humanity, but became man for men's sake.

Immanent Righteousness

It is one of the most surprising experiences, but at the same time one of the most incontrovertible, that evil —often in a surprisingly short time—proves its own folly and defeats its own object. That does not mean that punishment follows hard on the heels of every evil action; but it does mean that deliberate transgression of the divine law in the supposed interests of worldly self-preservation has exactly the opposite effect. We learn this from our own experience, and we can interpret it in various ways. At least it seems possible to infer with certainty that in social life there are laws more powerful than anything that may claim to dominate them, and that it is therefore not only wrong but unwise to disregard them. We can understand from this why Aristotelian-Thomist ethics made wisdom one of the cardinal virtues. Wisdom and folly are not ethically indifferent, as Neo-protestant motive-ethics[1] would have it. In the fullness of the concrete situation and the possibilities which it offers, the wise man at the same time recognizes the impassable limits that are set to all action by the permanent laws of human social life; and in this knowledge the wise man acts well and the good man wisely.

It is true that all historically important action is constantly overstepping the limits set by these laws. But it makes all the difference whether such overstepping of the appointed limits is regarded in principle as the superseding of them, and is therefore given out to be a law of a special kind, or whether the overstepping is deliberately regarded as a fault which is perhaps unavoidable, justified only if the law and the limit are re-established and respected as soon as possible. It is not necessarily hypocrisy if the declared aim of political action is the restoration of the law, and not mere self-preservation. The world is, in fact, so ordered that a basic respect for ultimate laws and human life is also the best means of self-preservation, and that these laws may be broken only on the odd occasion in case of brief necessity, whereas anyone who turns necessity into

[1] German *Gesinnungsethik*: "A view of ethics in which men's attitudes (the motives of their actions), rather than their actions, are moral or immoral." F. Aufsteda, *Kleines Wörterbuch der Philosophie* (Frankfurt-Main, 1954), 68.

a principle, and in so doing establishes a law of his own alongside them, is inevitably bound, sooner or later, to suffer retribution. The immanent righteousness of history rewards and punishes only men's deeds, but the eternal righteousness of God tries and judges their hearts.

A Few Articles of Faith on the Sovereignty of God in History

I believe that God can and will bring good out of evil, even out of the greatest evil. For that purpose he needs men who make the best use of everything. I believe that God will give us all the strength we need to help us to resist in all time of distress. But he never gives it in advance, lest we should rely on ourselves and not on him alone. A faith such as this should allay all our fears for the future. I believe that even our mistakes and shortcomings are turned to good account, and that it is no harder for God to deal with them than with our supposedly good deeds. I believe that God is no timeless fate, but that he waits for and answers sincere prayers and responsible actions.

Confidence

There is hardly one of us who has not known what it is to be betrayed. The figure of Judas, which we used to find so difficult to understand, is now fairly familiar to us. The air that we breathe is so polluted by mistrust that it almost chokes us. But where we have broken through the layer of mistrust, we have been able to discover a confidence hitherto undreamed of. Where we trust, we have learnt to put our very lives into the hands of others; in the face of all the different interpretations that have been put on our lives and actions, we have learnt to trust unreservedly. We now know that only such confidence, which is always a venture, though a glad and positive venture, enables us really to live and

work. We know that it is most reprehensible to sow
and encourage mistrust, and that our duty is rather to
foster and strengthen confidence wherever we can.
Trust will always be one of the greatest, rarest, and
happiest blessings of our life in a community, though it
can emerge only on the dark background of a necessary mistrust. We have learnt never to trust a scoundrel
an inch, but to give ourselves to the trustworthy without reserve.

The Sense of Quality

Unless we have the courage to fight for a revival of
wholesome reserve between man and man, we shall
perish in an anarchy of human values. The impudent
contempt for such reserve is the mark of the rabble,
just as inward uncertainty, haggling and cringing for
the favour of insolent people, and lowering oneself to
the level of the rabble are the way of becoming no better than the rabble itself. When we forget what is due
to ourselves and to others, when the feeling for human
quality and the power to exercise reserve cease to exist,
chaos is at the door. When we tolerate impudence for
the sake of material comforts, then we abandon our
self-respect, the flood-gates are opened, chaos bursts
the dam that we were to defend; and we are responsible
for it all. In other times it may have been the business
of Christianity to champion the equality of all men; its
business today will be to defend passionately human
dignity and reserve. The misinterpretation that we are
acting for our own interests, and the cheap insinuation
that our attitude is anti-social, we shall simply have to
put up with; they are the invariable protests of the rabble against decency and order. Anyone who is pliant
and uncertain in this matter does not realize what is at
stake, and indeed in his case the reproaches may well
be justified. We are witnessing the levelling down of all
ranks of society, and at the same time the birth of a

new sense of nobility, which is binding together a circle of men from all former social classes. Nobility arises from and exists by sacrifice, courage, and a clear sense of duty to oneself and society, by expecting due regard for itself as a matter of course; and it shows an equally natural regard for others, whether they are of higher or of lower degree. We need all along the line to recover the lost sense of quality and a social order based on quality. Quality is the greatest enemy of any kind of mass-levelling. Socially it means the renunciation of all place-hunting, a break with the cult of the "star," an open eye both upwards and downwards, especially in the choice of one's more intimate friends, and pleasure in private life as well as courage to enter public life. Culturally it means a return from the newspaper and the radio to the book, from feverish activity to unhurried leisure, from dispersion to concentration, from sensationalism to reflection, from virtuosity to art, from snobbery to modesty, from extravagance to moderation. Quantities are competitive, qualities are complementary.

Sympathy

We must allow for the fact that most people learn wisdom only by personal experience. This explains, first, why so few people are capable of taking precautions in advance—they always fancy that they will somehow or other avoid the danger, till it is too late. Secondly, it explains their insensibility to the sufferings of others; sympathy grows in proportion to the fear of approaching disaster. There is a good deal of excuse on ethical grounds for this attitude. No one wants to meet fate head-on; inward calling and strength for action are acquired only in the actual emergency. No one is responsible for all the injustice and suffering in the world, and no one wants to set himself up as the judge of the world. Psychologically, our lack of imagination, of sensitivity, and of mental alertness is balanced by a steady composure, an ability to go on working, and a great capacity for suffering. But from a Christian point of view, none of these excuses can obscure the fact that the most important factor, large-heartedness, is lacking. Christ kept himself from suffering till his hour had come, but when it did come he met it as a free man, seized it, and mastered it. Christ, so the Scriptures tell us, bore the sufferings of all humanity in his own body as if they were his own—a thought beyond our comprehension—accepting them of his own free will. We are certainly not Christ; we are not called on to redeem the world by our own deeds and sufferings, and we need not try to assume such an impossible burden. We are not lords, but instruments in the hand of the Lord of history; and we can share in other people's sufferings only in a very limited degree. We are not Christ, but if we want to be Christians, we must have some share in Christ's large-heartedness by acting with responsibility and in freedom when the hour of danger comes, and by showing a real sympathy that springs, not from fear, but from the liberating and redeeming love of Christ for all who suffer. Mere waiting and looking on is not Christian behaviour. The Christian is called to sympathy and action, not in the first place by his own sufferings, but by the sufferings of his brethren, for whose sake Christ suffered.

Of Suffering

It is infinitely easier to suffer in obedience to a human command than in the freedom of one's own responsibility. It is infinitely easier to suffer with others than to suffer alone. It is infinitely easier to suffer publicly and honourably than apart and ignominiously. It is infinitely easier to suffer through staking one's life than to suffer spiritually. Christ suffered as a free man alone, apart and in ignominy, in body and spirit; and since then many Christians have suffered with him.

Present and Future

We used to think that one of the inalienable rights of man was that he should be able to plan both his professional and his private life. That is a thing of the past. The force of circumstances has brought us into a situation where we have to give up being "anxious about tomorrow" (Matt. 6.34). But it makes all the difference whether we accept this willingly and in faith (as the Sermon on the Mount intends), or under continual constraint. For most people, the compulsory abandonment of planning for the future means that they are forced back into living just for the moment, irresponsibly, frivolously, or resignedly; some few dream longingly of better times to come, and try to forget the present. We find both these courses equally impossible, and there remains for us only the very narrow way, often extremely difficult to find, of living every day as if it were our last, and yet living in faith and responsibility as though there were to be a great future: "Houses and fields and vineyards shall again be bought in this land" proclaims Jeremiah (32.15), in paradoxical contrast to his prophecies of woe, just before the destruction of the holy city. It is a sign from God and a pledge of a fresh start and a great future, just when all seems black. Thinking and acting for the sake of the coming generation, but being ready to go any day without fear or anxiety—that, in practice, is the spirit in which we are forced to live. It is not easy to be brave and keep that spirit alive, but it is imperative.

Optimism

It is wiser to be pessimistic; it is a way of avoiding disappointment and ridicule, and so wise people con-

demn optimism. The essence of optimism is not its
view of the present, but the fact that it is the inspiration of life and hope when others give in; it enables a
man to hold his head high when everything seems to be
going wrong; it gives him strength to sustain reverses
and yet to claim the future for himself instead of abandoning it to his opponent. It is true that there is a silly,
cowardly kind of optimism, which we must condemn.
But the optimism that is will for the future should never
be despised, even if it is proven wrong a hundred times;
it is health and vitality, and the sick man has no business to impugn it. There are people who regard it as
frivolous, and some Christians think it impious for anyone to hope and prepare for a better earthly future.
They think that the meaning of present events is chaos,
disorder, and catastrophe; and in resignation or pious
escapism they surrender all responsibility for recon-
struction and for future generations. It may be that the
day of judgment will dawn tomorrow; and in that case,
though not before, we shall gladly stop working for a
better future.

Insecurity and death

In recent years we have become increasingly familiar
with the thought of death. We surprise ourselves by the
calmness with which we hear of the death of one of our
contemporaries. We cannot hate it as we used to, for
we have discovered some good in it, and have almost
come to terms with it. Fundamentally we feel that we
really belong to death already, and that every new day
is a miracle. It would probably not be true to say that
we welcome death (although we all know that weari-
ness which we ought to avoid like the plague); we are
too inquisitive for that—or, to put it more seriously, we
should like to see something more of the meaning of
our life's broken fragments. Nor do we try to romanti-
cize death, for life is too great and too precious. Still

less do we suppose that danger is the meaning of life—
we are not desperate enough for that, and we know too
much about the good things that life has to offer, though
on the other hand we are only too familiar with life's
anxieties and with all the other destructive effects of
prolonged personal insecurity. We still love life, but I
do not think that death can take us by surprise now.
After what we have been through during the war, we
hardly dare admit that we should like death to come to
us, not accidentally and suddenly through some trivial
cause, but in the fullness of life and with everything at
stake. It is we ourselves, and not outward circumstances, who make death what it can be, a death freely
and voluntarily accepted.

Are we still of any use?

We have been silent witnesses of evil deeds; we have
been drenched by many storms; we have learnt the arts
of equivocation and pretence; experience has made us
suspicious of others and kept us from being truthful
and open; intolerable conflicts have worn us down and
even made us cynical. Are we still of any use? What
we shall need is not geniuses, or cynics, or mis-
anthropes, or clever tacticians, but plain, honest,
straightforward men. Will our inward power of resistance be strong enough, and our honesty with ourselves
remorseless enough, for us to find our way back to
simplicity and straightforwardness?

2

LETTERS TO HIS PARENTS

14 April 1943

My dear Parents,

I DO WANT you to be quite sure that I am all right. I am sorry that I was not allowed to write to you sooner, but I was all right during the first ten days too. Strangely enough, the discomforts that one generally associates with prison life, the physical hardships, hardly bother me at all. One can even have enough to eat in the mornings with dry bread (I get a variety of extras too). The hard prison bed does not worry me a bit, and one can get plenty of sleep between 8 p.m. and 6 a.m. I have been particularly surprised that I have hardly felt any need at all for cigarettes since I came here; but I think that in all this the psychic factor has played the larger part. A violent mental upheaval such as is produced by a sudden arrest brings with it the need to take one's mental bearings and come to terms with an entirely new situation—all this means that physical things take a back seat and lose their importance, and it is something that I find to be a real enrichment of my experience. I am not so unused to being alone as other people are, and it is certainly a good spiritual Turkish bath. The only thing that bothers me or would bother me is the thought that you are being tormented by anxiety about me, and are not sleeping or eating properly. Forgive me for causing you so much worry, but I think a hostile fate is more to blame than I am. To set off against that, it is good to read Paul Gerhardt's hymns and learn them by heart, as I am doing now. Besides that, I have my Bible and some reading matter from the library here, and enough writing paper now. . . .

The 75th birthday[1] celebrations were a fortnight ago today. It was a splendid day. I can still hear the hymns that we sang in the morning and evening, with all the voices and instruments: "Praise to the Lord, the Almighty, the King of Creation. . . . Shelters thee under his wings, yea, and gently sustaineth."[2] That is true, and it is what we must always rely on. Spring is really coming now. You will have plenty to do in the garden. Here in the prison yard there is a thrush which sings beautifully in the morning, and now in the evening too. One is grateful for little things, and that is surely a gain. Good-bye for now.

Easter Day,
25 April 1943

At last the tenth day has come round, and I am allowed to write to you again; and I am so glad to let you know that even here I am having a happy Easter. Good Friday and Easter free us to think about other things far beyond our own personal fate, about the ultimate meaning of all life, suffering, and events; and we lay hold of a great hope. Since yesterday it has been marvellously quiet in the house. I heard many people wishing each other a happy Easter, and one does not begrudge it anyone who is on duty here—it's a hard job.

First of all, I must thank you very much for all the

---

[1] Of his father, Dr. Karl Bonhoeffer.
[2] From "*Lobe den Herren* . . ." by Joachim Neander.

things that you brought me. . . . You can't imagine what it means to be suddenly told: "Your mother and sister and brother have just been here, and they've left something for you." The mere fact that you have been near me, the tangible evidence that you are still thinking and caring about me (which of course I really know anyway!) is enough to keep me happy for the rest of the day. Thank you very much indeed for everything.

Things are still all right, and I am well. I am allowed out of doors for half an hour every day, and now that I can smoke again, I even forget sometimes, for a little while, where I am! I am being treated well, and I read a good deal—newspapers, novels, and above all the Bible. I can't concentrate enough yet for serious work, but during Holy Week I at last managed to work solidly through a part of the Passion story that has occupied me a great deal for a long time—the high-priestly prayer of our Lord. I have even been able to expound to myself a few chapters of Pauline ethical material; I felt that to be very important. So I really have a great deal to be very thankful for.

It is surprising how quickly the days pass here. I can hardly believe that I have been here three weeks. I like going to bed at eight o'clock (supper is at four), and I look forward to my dreams. I never knew before what a source of pleasure that can be; I dream every day, and always about something pleasant. Before I go to sleep I repeat to myself the verses that I have learnt during the day, and at 6 a.m. I like to read psalms and hymns, think of you all, and know that you are thinking of me.—The day is over now, and I hope you are feeling as peaceful as I am. I have read a lot of good things, and my thoughts and hopes have been pleasant too.

5 May 1943

I have now had four weeks in prison; and whereas I was able from the outset to accept my lot consciously, I am now getting used to it in a kind of natural and unconscious way. That is a relief, but it raises problems of its own, for one rightly does not want to get used to being in this position; I think you will feel the same way about it.—You want to know more about my life here. To picture to oneself a cell does not need much imagination—the less you use, the nearer the mark you will be. At Easter the *Deutsche Allgemeine Zeitung* brought out a reproduction from Dürer's *Apocalypse*, which I pinned up on the wall; and some of M's[3] primulas are still here too. Our day lasts fourteen hours, of which I spend about three walking up and down the cell—several miles a day, besides half an hour in the yard. I read, learn, and work. I particularly enjoyed reading Gotthelf again, with his clear, wholesome, serene style. I am getting on all right and keeping well.

The wedding at S's[4] will soon be here now, and I shall not be able to write again before then. I have lately been reading in Jean Paul that "the only joys that can stand the fires of adversity are the joys of home." . . . I wish you a happy day from the bottom of my heart, and I shall be with you in spirit with all happy thoughts and wishes. May you think of me, too, only with happy memories and hopes. It is when life goes hard that we particularly want to feel the real joys of life too—and a wedding is certainly one of them. . . .

I often think here of that lovely song of Hugo Wolf's, which we have sung several times lately:

> *Über Nacht, über Nacht*
> *kommt Freud und Leid*
> *und eh du's gedacht,*

[3] Maria von Wedemeyer, Bonhoeffer's fiancée.
[4] The Schleichers, the family of Bonhoeffer's eldest sister. The wedding was of Eberhard Bethge and Renate Schleicher.

verlassen dich beid',
und gehen dem Herren zu sagen,
wie du sie getragen.[5]

It all turns on that "how," which is more important than anything that happens to you from outside. It allays all the anxieties about the future which sometimes torment us. Thank you again very much for remembering me every day, and for all that you are doing and putting up with on my account. My best wishes to the family and friends. Tell R. to have a really happy wedding with no sad thoughts, and to rest assured that even here I can join in all her happiness.

15 May 1943

By the time you get this letter, all the final preparations and the wedding itself will be over, as will my own bit of longing to be there myself. . . . I am looking back today in gratitude for the happy times that we have had, and am happy about them all. I am anxious to hear what the text of the sermon was; the best I can think of is Romans 15.7, a text that I have often used myself. What splendid summer weather they are having; I expect this morning's hymn was Paul Gerhardt's *Die güldne Sonne.*

Your letter has taken some time to come. . . . Many thanks for it. Anyone for whom the parental home has become so much a part of himself as it has for me feels specially grateful for any message from home. If only we could see each other or talk together for a short time, what a great relief it would be.

Of course, people outside find it difficult to imagine what prison life is like. The situation in itself—that is each single moment—is perhaps not so very different here from anywhere else; I read, meditate, write, pace

[5] "Over night, over night, come joy and sorrow, and before you know it, both leave you and go to the Lord, to say how you have borne them."

up and down my cell—without rubbing myself sore against the walls like a polar bear. The great thing is to stick to what one still has and can do—there is still plenty left—and not to be dominated by the thought of what one cannot do, and by feelings of resentment and discontent. I am sure I never realized as clearly as I do here what the Bible and Luther mean by "temptation." Quite suddenly, and for no apparent physical or psychological reason, the peace and composure that were supporting one are jarred, and the heart becomes, in Jeremiah's expressive phrase, "deceitful above all things, and desperately corrupt; who can understand it?" It feels like an invasion from outside, as if by evil powers trying to rob one of what is most vital. But no doubt these experiences are good and necessary, as they teach one to understand human life better. I am just trying my hand at a little essay on "The feeling of time," a thing that is specially relevant to anyone who is being held for examination. One of my predecessors here has scribbled over the cell door, "In 100 years it will all be over." That was his way of trying to counter the feeling that life spent here is a blank; but there is a great deal that might be said about that, and I should like to talk it over with Father. "My times are in thy hand" (Ps. 31.15) is the Bible's answer. But in the Bible there is also the question that threatens to dominate everything here: "How long, O Lord?" (Ps. 13). . . .

By the way, you really ought to read J. Gotthelf's *Berner Geist*, and if not the whole of it, at least the first part; it is something out of the ordinary, and it will certainly interest you. I remember how old Dr. Schöne[6] always had a special word of praise for Gotthelf, and I should like to suggest to the Diederich Press that they bring out a Gotthelf day-book. Stifter's background,

---

[6] Richard Schöne, the Bonhoeffers' neighbour in Grunewald, and former director of the Berlin museums.

too, is mainly Christian; his woodland scenes often make me long to be back again in the quiet glades of Friedrichsbrunn. He is not so forceful as Gotthelf, but he is wonderfully clear and simple, and that gives me a great deal of pleasure. If only we could talk to each other about these things. For all my sympathy with the contemplative life, I am not a born Trappist. Of course, a period of enforced silence may be a good thing, and the Roman Catholics say that the most effective expositions of Scripture come from the purely contemplative orders. I am reading the Bible straight through from cover to cover, and have just got as far as Job, which I am particularly fond of. I read the Psalms every day, as I have done for years; I know them and love them more than any other book. I cannot now read Psalms 3, 47, 70, and others without hearing them in the settings by Heinrich Schütz. It was R.[7] who introduced me to his music, and I count it one of the greatest enrichments of my life.

. . . I feel myself so much a part of you all that I know that we live and bear everything in common, acting and thinking for one another, even though we have to be separated.

[7] R(enate) here means Eberhard Bethge.

3

A WEDDING SERMON FROM A
PRISON CELL

(May 1943)

*Eph. 1.12: "We who . . . have been destined and ap-
pointed to live for the praise of his glory."*

IT IS RIGHT and proper for a bride and bridegroom to
welcome and celebrate their wedding day with a unique
sense of triumph. When all the difficulties, obstacles,
hindrances, doubts, and misgivings have been, not
made light of, but honestly faced and overcome—and
it is certainly better not to take everything for granted
—then both parties have indeed achieved the most important triumph of their lives. With the "Yes"[1] that
they have said to each other, they have by their free
choice given a new direction to their lives; they have
cheerfully and confidently defied all the uncertainties
and hesitations with which, as they know, a lifelong
partnership between two people is faced; and by their
own free and responsible action they have conquered a
new land to live in. Every wedding must be an occasion
of joy that human beings can do such great things, that

---

[1] In the German wedding ceremony the bride and bridegroom say "Yes," not "I will."

they have been given such immense freedom and power to take the helm in their life's journey. The children of the earth are rightly proud of being allowed to take a hand in shaping their own destinies, and something of this pride must contribute to the happiness of a bride and bridegroom. We ought not to be in too much of a hurry here to speak piously of God's will and guidance. It is obvious, and it should not be ignored, that it is your own very human wills that are at work here, celebrating their triumph; the course that you are taking at the outset is one that you have chosen for yourselves; what you have done and are doing is not, in the first place, something religious, but something quite secular. So you yourselves, and you alone, bear the responsibility for what no one can take from you; or, to put it more exactly, it is you, the bride and bridegroom, on whom the whole responsibility is laid for the success of your venture, with all the happiness that such responsibility involves. Unless you can boldly say today: "This is *our* resolve, *our* love, *our* way," you are taking refuge in a false piety. "Iron and steel may pass away, but *our* love shall abide for ever." That desire for earthly bliss, which you want to find in one another, and in which, to quote the medieval song, one is the comfort of the other both in body and in soul—that desire is justified before God and man.

Certainly you two, of all people, have every reason to look back with special thankfulness on your lives up to now. The beautiful things and the joys of life have been showered on you, you have succeeded in everything, and you have been surrounded by love and friendship. Your ways have, for the most part, been smoothed before you took them, and you have always been able to count on the support of your families and friends. Everyone has wished you well, and now it has been given to you to find each other and to reach the goal of your desires. You yourselves know that no one can create and assume such a life from his own strength, but that what is given to one is withheld from another; and that is what we call God's guidance. So today, however much you rejoice that you have reached your goal, you will be just as thankful that God's will and God's way have brought you here; and however confidently you accept responsibility for your action today, you may and will put it today with equal confidence into God's hands.

As God today adds his "Yes" to your "Yes," as he confirms your will with his will, and as he allows you, and approves of, your triumph and rejoicing and pride, he makes you at the same time instruments of his will and purpose both for yourselves and for others. In his unfathomable condescension God does add his "Yes" to yours; but by doing so, he creates out of your love something quite new—the holy estate of matrimony.

God is guiding your marriage. Marriage is more than your love for each other. It has a higher dignity and power, for it is God's holy ordinance, through which he wills to perpetuate the human race till the end of time. In your wedding you see only your two selves in the world, but in marriage you are a link in the chain of the generations, which God causes to come and to pass away to his glory, and calls into his kingdom. In your love you see only the heaven of your happiness, but in marriage you are placed at a post of responsibility towards the world and mankind. Your love is your own private possession, but marriage is more than something personal—it is a status, an office. Just as it is the crown, and not merely the will to rule, that makes the king, so it is marriage, and not merely your love for each other, that joins you together in the sight of God and man. As you first gave the ring to one another and have now received it a second time from the hand of the pastor, so love comes from you, but marriage from above, from God. As high as God is above man, so high are the

sanctity, the rights, and the promise of marriage above
the sanctity, the rights, and the promise of love. It is
not your love that sustains the marriage, but from now
on, the marriage that sustains your love.

God makes your marriage indissoluble. "What therefore God has joined together, let no man put asunder"
(Matt. 19.6). God joins you together in marriage; it is
his act, not yours. Do not confound your love for one
another with God. God makes your marriage indissoluble, and protects it from every danger that may threaten
it from within and without; he will be the guarantor of
its indissolubility. It is a blessed thing to know that no
power on earth, no temptation, no human frailty can
dissolve what God holds together; indeed, anyone who
knows that may say confidently: What God has joined
together, *can* no man put asunder. Free from all the
anxiety that is always a characteristic of love, you can
now say to each other with complete and confident assurance: We can never lose each other now; by the will
of God we belong to each other till death.

*God establishes a rule of life by which you can live
together in wedlock:* "Wives, be subject to your husbands, as is fitting in the Lord. Husbands, love your
wives." (Col. 3.18, 19). With your marriage you are
founding a home. That needs a rule of life, and this
rule of life is so important that God establishes it himself, because without it everything would get out of
joint. You may order your home as you like, except in
one thing: the wife is to be subject to her husband, and
the husband is to love his wife. In this way God gives
to husband and wife the honour that is due to each.
The wife's honour is to serve the husband, to be a
"help meet for him," as the creation story has it (Gen.
2.18); and the husband's honour is to love his wife
with all his heart. He will "leave his father and mother
and be joined to his wife" (Matt. 19.5), and will "love
her as his own flesh." A wife who wants to dominate

her husband dishonours herself and him, just as a husband who does not love his wife as he should dishonours himself and her; and both dishonour the glory of
God that is meant to rest on the estate of matrimony.
It is an unhealthy state of affairs when the wife's ambi-
tion is to be like the husband, and the husband regards
the wife merely as the plaything of his own lust for
power and licence; and it is a sign of social disintegration when the wife's service is felt to be degrading or
beneath her dignity, and when the husband who is faithful to his wife is looked on as a weakling or even a
fool.

The place where God has put the wife is the husband's home. Most people have forgotten nowadays
what a home can mean, though some of us have come
to realize it as never before. It is a kingdom of its own
in the midst of the world, a stronghold amid life's
storms and stresses, a refuge, even a sanctuary. It is not
founded on the shifting sands of outward or public life,
but it has its peace in God, for it is God who gives it
its special meaning and value, its own nature and privilege, its own destiny and dignity. It is an ordinance of
God in the world, the place in which—whatever may
happen in the world—peace, quietness, joy, love,
purity, discipline, respect, obedience, tradition, and,
with it all, happiness may dwell. It is the wife's calling,
and her happiness, to build up for her husband this
world within the world, and to do her life's work there.
How happy she is if she realizes how great and rich a
task and destiny she has. Not novelty, but permanence,
not change, but constancy, not noisiness, but peace, not
words, but deeds, not commands, but persuasion, not
desire, but possession—and all these things inspired and
sustained by her love for her husband—, that is the
wife's kingdom. In the Book of Proverbs we read
(31.11 ff.): "The heart of her husband trusts in her,
and he will have no lack of gain. She does him good,

and not harm, all the days of her life. She seeks wool
and flax, and works with willing hands. . . . She rises
while it is yet night and provides food for her household
and tasks for her maidens. . . . She opens her hand to
the poor, and reaches our her hands to the needy. . . .
Strength and dignity are her clothing, and she laughs
at the time to come. . . . Her children rise up and call
her blessed; her husband also, and he praises her. . . .
Many women have done excellently, but you surpass
them all." Again and again the Bible praises, as the
supreme earthly happiness, the fortune of a man who
finds a true, or as the Bible puts it, a "virtuous" or
"wise" woman. "She is far more precious then jewels"
(Prov. 31.10). "A virtuous woman is the crown of her
husband" (Prov. 12.4). But the Bible speaks just as
frankly of the mischief that a perverse, "foolish" woman
brings on her husband and her home.

Now when the husband is called "the head of the
wife," and it goes on to say "as Christ is the head of
the church" (Eph. 5.23), something of the divine
splendour is reflected in our earthly relationships, and
this reflection we should recognize and honour. The
dignity that is here ascribed to the man lies, not in any
capacities or qualities of his own, but in the office con-
ferred on him by his marriage. The wife should see her
husband clothed in this dignity. But for him it is a supreme responsibility. As the head, it is he who is responsible for his wife, for their marriage, and for their
home. On him falls the care and protection of the family; he represents it to the outside world; he is its main-
stay and comfort; he is the master of the house, who
exhorts, punishes, helps, and comforts, and stands for
it before God. It is a good thing, for it is a divine ordinance when the wife honours the husband for his office's sake, and when the husband properly performs
the duties of his office. The husband and wife who acknowledge and observe God's ordinance are "wise,"

but those who think to replace it by another of their own devising are "foolish."

God has laid on marriage a blessing and a burden. The blessing is the promise of children. God allows man to share in his continual work of creation; but it is always God himself who blesses marriage with children. "Children are a heritage from the Lord" (Psalm 127.3), and they should be acknowledged as such. It is from God that parents receive their children, and it is to God that they should lead them. Parents therefore have divine authority in respect to their children. Luther speaks of the "golden chain" with which God invests parents; and Scripture adds to the fifth commandment the special promise of long life on earth. Since men live on earth, God has given them a lasting reminder that this earth stands under the curse of sin and is not itself the ultimate reality. Over the destiny of woman and of man lies the dark shadow of a word of God's wrath, a burden from God, which they must carry. The woman must bear her children in pain, and in providing for his family the man must reap many thorns and thistles, and labour in the sweat of his brow. This burden should cause both man and wife to call on God, and should remind them of their eternal destiny in his kingdom. Earthly society is only the beginning of the heavenly society, the earthly home an image of the heavenly home, the earthly family a symbol of the fatherhood of God over all men, for they are his children.

God gives you Christ as the foundation of your marriage. "Welcome one another, therefore, as Christ has welcomed you, for the glory of God" (Rom. 15.7). In a word, live together in the forgiveness of your sins, for without it no human fellowship, least of all a marriage, can survive. Don't insist on your rights, don't blame each other, don't judge or condemn each other, don't find fault with each other, but accept each other as you are, and forgive each other every day from the bottom of your hearts.

From the first day of your wedding till the last the rule must be: "Welcome one another . . . for the glory of God."

That is God's word for your marriage. Thank him for it; thank him for leading you thus far; ask him to establish your marriage, to confirm it, sanctify it, and preserve it. So your marriage will be "for the praise of his glory." Amen.

4

LETTERS TO HIS PARENTS

Ascension Day,
4 June 1943

THANK YOU VERY much for your letters. They are always too short for *me*, but of course I understand! It is as though the prison gates were opened for a moment, and I could share a little of your life outside. Joy is a thing that we want very badly in this solemn building, where one never hears a laugh—it seems to get even the warders down—and we exhaust all our reserves of it from within and without.

Today is Ascension Day, and that means that it is a day of great joy for all who can believe that Christ rules the world and our lives. My thoughts go out to all of you, to the Church and its services, from which I have now been separated for so long, and also to the many unknown people in this building who are bearing their fate in silence. I repeatedly find that these and other thoughts keep me from taking my own little hardships too seriously; that would be very wrong and ungrateful.

I have just written a little more about "The feeling of time"; I am very much enjoying it, and when we write from personal experience, we can write more fluently and freely. Thank you very much, Father, for

Kant's *Anthropologie*, which I have read through; I did not know it. There was a great deal that was interesting in it, but it has a very rationalist rococo psychology, which simply ignores many essential phenomena. Can you send me something good about forms and functions of memory? It is a thing that interests me very much in this connection. Kant's exposition of "smoking" as a means of entertaining oneself is very nice.

I am very glad that you are now reading Gotthelf; I am sure you would like his *Wanderungen* . . . just as much. For serious reading I have been very glad to read here Ulhorn's great *Geschichte der christlichen Liebestätigkeit*; Holl's *Kirchengeschichte* reminds me of his seminars.

I read some of Stifter almost every day. The intimate life of his characters—of course it is old-fashioned of him to describe only likable people—is very pleasant in this atmosphere here, and makes one think of the things that really matter in life. Prison life in general brings one back, both outwardly and inwardly, to the simplest things of life; that explains why I could not get on at all with Rilke. But I wonder whether one's understanding is not affected by the restrictive nature of life here. . . .

Whitsunday,
14 June 1943

Well, Whitsuntide is here, and we are still separated; but it is in a special way a feast of fellowship. When the bells rang this morning, I longed to go to church, but instead I did as John did on the island of Patmos, and had such a splendid service of my own, that I did not feel lonely at all, for you were all with me, every one of you, and so were the congregations in whose company I have kept Whitsuntide. Every hour or so since yesterday evening I have been repeating to my own comfort Paul Gerhardt's Whitsun hymn with the lovely lines "Thou art a Spirit of joy" and "Grant us joyfulness and strength," and besides that, the words "If you faint in the day of adversity, your strength is small" (Prov. 24), and "God did not give us a spirit of timidity but a spirit of power and love and self-control" (II Tim. 1). I have also been considering again the strange story of the gift of tongues. That the confusion of tongues at the Tower of Babel, as a result of which people can no longer understand each other, because everyone speaks a different language, should at last be brought to an end and overcome by the language of God, which everyone understands and through which alone people can understand each other again, and that the Church should be the place where that happens—these are great momentous thoughts. Leibniz grappled all his life with the idea of a universal script consisting, not of words, but of self-evident signs representing every possible idea. It was an expression of his wish to heal the world, which was then so torn to pieces, a philosophical reflection on the Pentecost story.—Once again all is silent here; one hears nothing but the tramp of the prisoners pacing up and down in their cells. How many comfortless and un-Whitsun-like thoughts there must be in their minds! If I were prison chaplain here, I should spend the whole time from morning till night on days like this, going through the cells; a good deal would happen. . . .

You are all waiting, just as I am, and I must admit that in some part or other of my subconscious mind I had been hoping to be out of here by Whitsuntide, although I am always deliberately telling myself not to envisage any particular date. It will be ten weeks tomorrow; as mere laymen we did not imagine that "temporary" confinement would amount to this. But after all, it is a mistake to be as unsuspecting in legal matters as I am; it brings home to one what a different atmosphere the lawyer must live in from the theologian;

but that is instructive too, and everything has its proper place. All we can do is to wait as patiently as may be, without getting bitter, and to trust that everyone is doing his best to clear things up as quickly as possible. Fritz Reuter puts it very well: "No one's life flows on such an even course that it does not sometimes come up against a dam and whirl round and round, or that people never throw stones into the clear water. Something happens to everyone, and he must take care that the water stays clear, and that heaven and earth are reflected in it"—when you have said that, you have really said everything. . . .

My essay on "The feeling of time" is practically finished; and now I am going to let it lie for a while and see what it looks like later.

It is Whitmonday, and I was just sitting down to a dinner of turnips and potatoes when your parcel that R[üdiger] brought as a Whitsuntide present arrived quite unexpectedly. I really cannot tell you what happiness such things give one. However certain I am of the spiritual bond between all of you and myself, the spirit always seems to want some visible token of this union of love and remembrance, and then material things become the vehicles of spiritual realities. I think this is analogous to the need felt in all religions for the visible appearance of the Spirit in the sacrament.

24 June 1943

What a blessing it is, in such distressing times, to belong to a large, closely knit family, where each trusts the other and stands by him. When pastors were arrested, I sometimes used to think that it must be easiest for those of them who were unmarried. But I did not know then what the warmth that radiates from the love of a wife and family can mean in the cold air of imprisonment, and how in just such times of separation the feeling of belonging together through thick and thin actually grows stronger. . . .

Some letters have just arrived, for which I thank you very much. From what you say about strawberries and raspberries, school holidays and plans for travel, I begin to feel that summer has really come. Time is not of much account here. I am glad the weather is mild. A little while ago a tomtit had its nest with its ten little ones in a recess in the yard here. I enjoyed going to look at it every day till some cruel fellow went and destroyed the lot and left some of the tomtits lying on the ground, dead; I can't understand it. When I walk in the yard I get a great deal of pleasure from a small ant-hill and from the bees in the lime-trees. I sometimes think of the story of Peter Bamm, who was on a lovely island where he met all kinds of people, good and bad. He dreamt in a nightmare that a bomb might come and destroy everything, and the first thing that occurred to him was what a pity it would be for the butterflies! Prison life brings home to one how nature carries on uninterruptedly its quiet, open life, and it gives one quite a special—perhaps a sentimental—attitude towards animal and plant life, except that my attitude towards the flies in my cell remains very unsentimental. In general, a prisoner is no doubt inclined to make up, through an exaggerated sentimentality, for the soullessness and lack of warmth in his surroundings; and perhaps he may react too strongly to anything sentimental that affects him personally. The right thing for him to do then is to call himself to order with a cold shower of common sense and humour, to avoid losing his sense of proportion. I believe it is just here that Christianity, rightly understood, can help particularly.

You, Father, know all this quite well from your long experience of prisoners. I am not yet sure what the so-called prison psychosis is, though I am getting a pretty good idea.

3 July 1943

When the bells of the prison chapel start ringing at about six o'clock on a Saturday evening, that is the best time to write home. It is remarkable what power church bells have over human beings, and how deeply they can affect us. So many of our life's experiences gather round them. All discontent, ingratitude, and selfishness melt away, and in a moment we are left with only our pleasant memories hovering round us like gracious spirits. I always think first of those quiet summer evenings in Friedrichsbrunn, then of all the different parishes that I have worked in, then of all our family occasions, weddings, christenings, and confirmations—tomorrow my godchild[1] is being confirmed!—I really cannot count all the memories that come alive to me, and they all inspire peace, thankfulness, and confidence. If only one could help other people more! During the past week I have done a good deal of quiet work, and have read some good books, as well as some letters from you; and now today there is your magnificent parcel. It makes me a bit uneasy that the windows of your air raid shelter are to be walled in. . . .

I have now been in prison three months. I remember hearing Schlatter say, in his lectures on ethics, that it was one of the duties of a Christian citizen to take it patiently if he were held for investigation. That meant nothing to me at the time, but in the past few weeks I have thought of it several times, and now we must wait calmly and patiently as long as we have to, just as we have done up to now. I am dreaming more than ever that I have been released and am back home with you. . . . The day lilies have been simply lovely; their cups open slowly in the morning and bloom only for a day;

[1] Marianne Leibholz, daughter of Bonhoeffer's twin sister Sabine Leibholz of Oxford.

and the next morning there are fresh ones to take their place. The day after tomorrow they will all be over.

Sunday,
25 July 1943

So you came here yesterday in all the heat to bring me the parcel! I hope it was not too much of an effort for you. Thank you very much for coming, and for all the things that you brought. The summer produce is particularly welcome here, of course. Fancy the tomatoes being ripe already! Just lately I have been feeling the warmth for the first time. It is not too uncomfortable here in the cell, especially as I keep fairly still most of the time. But one longs more and more for fresh air. I should just like to spend an evening in the garden again. Of course, it is nice to have half an hour's walking every day, but it is not enough. I suppose the various things associated with a cold—aches, catarrah, and so on—will not go till I can get into the fresh air again. The flowers are always a great blessing; they bring some colour and life into this dreary cell. . . .

In my reading I am now concentrating entirely on the nineteenth century. During recent months I have read Gotthelf, Stifter, Immermann, Fontane, and Keller with sheer admiration. A period in which people could write such clear and simple German must have had quite a healthy core. They treat the most delicate matters without sentimentality, the most serious without flippancy, and they express their convictions without pathos; there is no exaggerated simplifying or complicating of language or subject matter; in short, it is all very much to my liking, and seems to me very sound. But it must have meant plenty of hard work at expressing themselves in good German, and therefore plenty of opportunity for quiet. By the way, the last Reuters were as fascinating as ever; I am delighted and surprised at their equipoise, which often extends to the language itself. An author's style is often enough to attract or repel the readers. . . .

Each time I write, I hope it will be my last letter to you from prison. Of course, this really becomes more likely every day; and one gradually gets sick of being here. I do so wish for all of us that we could have a few more of the lovely summer days together.

3 August 1943

I am really very happy and thankful that I can write to you more often now, for I am afraid you must be worrying about me, first because of the heat in my cell just under the roof, and secondly because of my asking for a lawyer. Your wonderful parcel has just come with tomatoes, apples, bottled fruit, thermos flask, etc., and the cooling salt, which is fantastic—I never knew there was such a thing. What trouble you have taken for me again. Please don't worry; I have often had to put up with worse heat in Italy, Africa, Spain, Mexico, and, almost the worst of all, in New York in July 1939; so I have a fairly good idea what to do about it. I do not eat or drink much, I sit quietly at my desk, and so manage to work unhindered. From time to time I refresh my body and soul with your lovely things. I don't want to ask to be moved to another floor, as that would not be fair to the other prisoner who would have to come into my cell, probably without such things as tomatoes; and besides, it does not make much difference whether the temperature in the cell is 34 or only 30.[2] I am very sorry that Hans[3] finds the heat so trying. One sees again and again how much easier it is to put up with a thing if one knows it cannot be changed, than if there seems to be a chance of relief round the corner.

---

[2] 93 or 86 Fahrenheit.
[3] Hans von Dohnanyi, in the Lehrterstrasse prison at the same time.

Regarding my request for a lawyer to defend me, I very much hope that this has not caused you any great anxiety, but that you are waiting, as I am, for things to take their course. You really must not imagine that I am uneasy or depressed. Of course, this has been a disappointment for me, as I suppose it has been for you too. But in a way I feel freer now that I know my case will soon be finally cleared up, after we have been kept waiting for so long. I am expecting more information any day. . . .

Once again I have been reading a number of good things. *Jürg Jenatsch* brought back youthful memories and gave me a good deal of pleasure and interest. On historical matters I found the work about the Venetians very instructive and arresting. Will you please send me some Fontane: *Frau Jenny Treibel, Irrungen, Wirrungen,* and *Stechlin*? This concentrated reading of the last few months will be very useful for my work; one often learns more about ethics from such books as these than from text-books. I like Reuter's *Kein Hüsung* as much as you do, Mother. I expect I have finished the Reuters now—or have you anything else particularly good? . . .

The other day I read this pretty verse in *Der Grüne Heinrich*:

> *Und durch den starken Wellengang*
> *der See, die gegen mich verschworen,*
> *geht mir von Euerem Gesang,*
> *wenn auch gedämpft, kein Ton verloren.*[4]

7 August 1943

. . . I wonder whether you are still very much occupied with air raid precautions. After all that has been in the papers lately, one cannot help thinking out the whole

---

[4] "And across the surging ocean that has conspired against me, not one note of your song is lost to me, although it is muffled."

matter afresh. I just remember that we talked once about the beams in the cellar and were rather doubtful about them; were not some alterations going to be made in the central beam? I wonder whether you are still thinking of it, and whether you can get anyone to help with the work. I think it might be very difficult now. How I should love to help you with it myself. Do tell me all about it; I am interested in every detail. . . .

I don't think I have told you that every day, when I get tired of reading and writing, I work on a chess problem; I enjoy it very much. If you come across some good little work on the subject, perhaps with set problems, I should be grateful; but don't put yourselves out over it; I shall manage all right. . . .

17 August 1943

. . . Above all, please don't worry about me more than you can help. I am keeping up my end, and my mind is quite calm. What a good thing it is to know from previous experience that we are really not upset at all by air raids. I am very glad that the law courts . . . are to stay in Berlin. . . . Anyway, you—like myself—have something better to do than to be thinking all the time about possible raids. Prison life gives one, almost as a matter of course, a certain detachment from the actions and excitements of the day. . . .

For the last fortnight I have been waiting in such uncertainty day by day that I hardly felt equal to any serious work; but I am going to try now to get down to some more writing. Some weeks ago I sketched the outlines of a play, but meanwhile I have realized that the material is not suitable for drama; and so I shall now try to rewrite it as a story. It is about the life of a family, and of course there is a good deal of autobiography mixed up in it. . . .

The death of the three young pastors[5] grieves me very much. I should be grateful if their relatives could be told in some way that I cannot write to them now; otherwise they would not understand my not doing so. Of all my pupils, those three were closest to me. It is a great loss, both for me personally and for the Church. More than thirty of my pupils must have fallen by now, and most of them were among my best. . . .

24 August 1943

Well, you had a rough passage last night. I was very relieved when the Captain sent word to me that you were all right. My cell is high up, and the window is kept wide open during alerts, so one has a very clear view of the ghastly firework display on the south side of the city; and without the least feeling of anxiety for myself, I do feel most strongly at such times how utterly absurd it is for me to be kept waiting here doing nothing. I thought the *Brüdergemeinde* text for this morning was most appropriate: "And I will give peace in the land, and you shall lie down, and none shall make you afraid" (Lev. 26.6).

On Sunday night I stupidly got gastric catarrah; yesterday I had a temperature, but today it is normal again. I have only just got up to write this letter, and shall be going straight back to bed as a precaution; I do not want to be ill on any account. As such cases are not catered for here, I was very glad of your rusks and a packet of biscuits that I kept by me for emergencies. A medical orderly also gave me some of his white bread, so I am getting along quite well. One ought to have something of the kind here in case of need, and perhaps also a small packet of semolina or oat flakes,

---

[5] Erich Klapproth, Ulrich Sander, and Gustav Seydel, who had studied under Bonhoeffer at Finkenwalde.

which could be cooked in the sick bay. By the time you get this letter, the whole thing will be over and done with. . . .

31 August 1943

. . . For the last few days I have again been able to work well and write a good deal. When I find myself back in the cell after a few hours of complete absorption in my work, it takes me a moment or two to get my bearings again. The fact of my being here is even now hard to credit, however much I get used to the external conditions. I find it quite interesting to watch this gradual process of accustoming and adapting myself. A week ago I was given a knife and fork for my meals —a new provision—and they seemed almost unnecessary, as it had become so much a matter of course for me to use a spoon for spreading my bread and so on. On the other hand, I think there are some things that are so irrational, e.g. the actual state of being in prison, that it is impossible, or at least very difficult, to get used to them. That kind of thing needs a conscious effort if it is to be accepted. I expect there are psychological works on the subject.

Delbrück's *Weltgeschichte* is very good reading, only it seems to me to be more a history of Germany. I have finished *Die Mikrobenjäger*, and enjoyed it very much. I have also been reading some more of Storm, though without being very much impressed by it on the whole. I hope you will bring me some more of Fontane or Stifter. . . .

5 September 1943

I don't think there is any need for us to compare notes about the night before last. I shall never forget looking through the cell window at the horrible night sky. I was very relieved to hear from the Captain the next morning that you were safe. . . . It is remarkable how we think at such times about the people that we should not like to live without, and almost or entirely forget about ourselves. It is only then that we feel how closely our own lives are bound up with other people's, and in fact how the centre of our own lives is outside ourselves, and how little we are separate entities. The "as though it were a part of me"[6] is perfectly true, as I have often felt after hearing that one of my colleagues or pupils had been killed. I think it is a literal fact of nature that human life extends far beyond our physical existence. Probably a mother feels this more strongly than anyone else. There are two passages in the Bible which always seem to me to sum the thing up. One is from Jeremiah 45: "Behold, what I have built I am breaking down, and what I have planted I am plucking up. . . . And do you seek great things for yourself? Seek them not . . . but I will give your life as a prize of war . . ."; and the other is from Psalm 60: "Thou hast made the land to quake, thou hast rent it open; repair its breaches, for it totters."

I wish you would let me know whether you have had the anti-shrapnel trench dug, and whether it would not be possible for you to have an exit made from the cellar to the trench. That is what Captain M.[7] has done. . . .

I am still getting on all right. I have been moved two floors lower because of the raids, and now it is very nice to have a direct view from my window on to the church towers. Last week I was able to write quite well again. The only thing I miss is open air exercise, on which I depend very much for any useful work. But it won't be long now, and that is the main thing. . . .

---

[6] *"als wär's ein Stück von mir"* from the soldier's song, *Ich hatt' einen Kameraden.*

[7] Captain Maetz, the commandant of the military prison in Tegel.

13 September 1943

Last time I said I should like to have more letters, and in the last few days I have been delighted to have a whole sheaf of them. I almost seem to be like Palmström,[8] who ordered "a quarter's mixed correspondence." But seriously, on a day when there are letters there is a very noticeable change from the usual monotony. Now that I have also been given permission to have visitors,[9] things really are looking up. After the tiresome postal delays of recent weeks I have felt very grateful for that. I was glad that you seemed to be looking a little better when you came, but what worries me most about the whole business is that this year you have missed the holiday that you so badly needed. You really must go away for a time before winter, and it would be best of all if I could go with you. . . .

It is a strange feeling to be so completely dependent on other people; but at least it teaches one to be grateful, and I hope I shall never forget that. In ordinary life we hardly realize that we receive a great deal more than we give, and that it is only with gratitude that life becomes rich. It is very easy to overestimate the importance of our own achievements in comparison with what we owe to others.

The stormy happenings in the world in the last few days[10] go right through one, and I wish I could be doing useful service somewhere or other, but at present that "somewhere" must be in the prison cell, and what I can do here makes its contribution in the unseen world, and even there the word "do" is quite un-

---

[8] A fictitious character in C. Morgenstern's poems *Die Galgenlieder*.

[9] (In the presence of a warder.)

[10] The Russian counter-offensive; Badoglio's agreement to surrender in Italy; air raids on Hamburg; evacuation of Berlin.

suitable. I sometimes think of Schubert's *Münnich* and his crusade.

For the rest, I am reading and writing as much as I can, and I am glad to say that I have never had a moment's boredom in the five months and more that I have been here. My time is always fully occupied, but in the background there is always the feeling, from morning till night, of waiting for something.

A few weeks ago I asked you to get me some books that have just been published: N. Hartmann's *Systematische Philosophie* and *Das Zeitalter des Marius und Sulla*, published by Diederich; now I should also like *Die deutsche Musik* by R. Benz. I should not like to miss these things, and I should be glad to be able to read them while I am still here. K[arl] F[riedrich] wrote about a book on physics, written for the general reader, and said he would send it to me. K[laus] too, sometimes discovers books that are worth reading. I have practically finished everything that I want to read here. I may have another try at Jean Paul's *Siebenkäs* or *Flegeljahre*; I have them in my room. I might not bring myself to read them later on, and there are many well-read people who think highly of him. In spite of several attempts, I have always found him too long-winded and affected. But as we are now in mid-September, I hope these wishes will already be out of date before they are fulfilled.

25 September 1943

I wish very much that one were told at the outset how long a business like this is likely to last. Even in my work here there is a good deal that I could have done differently and more profitably. In fact, people being as they are, every week, every day is precious. Although it may sound paradoxical, I was really glad yesterday when at last permission for a lawyer[11] and then the

[11] Dr. Kurt Wergin.

warrant for my arrest came. So it seems that the apparently purposeless waiting will soon be over. At the same time, being in custody for so long has brought me experiences that I shall never forget. . . . For the rest, I am doing some writing, and noticing that I also enjoy doing free-lance, non-theological writing. But I am realizing for the first time how difficult the German language is, and how easily one can murder it. . . .

On reading this letter through, I think it sounds a bit disgruntled. That is not what I intend, and it would not represent my state of mind. Much as I long to be out of here, I don't believe a single day has been wasted. What will come out of my time here it is still too early to say; but something will come of it. . . .

4 October 1943

. . . Outside it is lovely autumn weather, and I wish that you—and I with you—were at Friedrichsbrunn, and also Hans and his family, who are all so specially fond of the cottage. But how many people must there be in the world today who cannot have their wishes met? I certainly don't agree with Diogenes that the greatest happiness is the absence of desire, and that the best place to live is in a tub; why should we be fooled into believing that kind of thing? But I do believe that it may be good for us, especially when we are young, to have to wait for what we want, although we ought not to go so far as to give up wishing for anything and grow apathetic. But I am in no danger of that at present. . . .

A letter from C.[12] has just come. It is surprising how he keeps thinking of writing. What a view of life a fourteen-year-old must get when he has to write to his father and godfather in prison for months on end. He cannot have many illusions about the world now; I sup-

---

[12] Christoph von Dohnanyi.

pose all these happenings mean the end of his child-hood. Please thank him very much for his letter; I am greatly looking forward to seeing him again.

I am glad you were able to get hold of Hartmann's *Systematische Philosophie*. I am getting down to it properly, and it will keep me busy for several weeks, if the interruption that I hope for does not occur in the meantime. . . .

13 October 1943

I have in front of me the gay bunch of dahlias that you brought me yesterday; it reminds me of the lovely hour that I was able to have with you, and of the garden, and in general of how beautiful the world can be in these autumn days. One of Storm's verses that I came across the other day just about expresses this mood, and keeps going through my head like a tune that one cannot get rid of:

> *Und geht es draussen noch so toll,*
> *unchristlich oder christlich,*
> *ist doch die Welt, die schöne Welt*
> *so gänzlich unverwüstlich.*[13]

All that is needed to bring that home to one is a few gay autumn flowers, the view from the cell window, and half an hour's "exercise" in the prison yard, where there are, in fact, a few beautiful chestnut and lime trees. But in the last resort, for me at any rate, the "world" consists of a few people whom I should like to see and to be with. . . . If, besides that, I could sometimes hear a good sermon on Sundays—I some-times hear fragments of the chorales that are carried along by the breeze—it would be still better. . . .

I have again been doing a good deal of writing lately,

[13] "And however crazy, or Christian, or unchristian things may be outside, this world, this beautiful world is quite in-destructible."

and for the work that I have set myself to do, the day is often too short, so that sometimes, comically enough, I even feel that I have "no time" here for this or that less important matter! After breakfast in the morning (about 7 o'clock) I read some theology, and then I write till midday; in the afternoon I read, then comes a chapter from Delbrück's *Weltgeschichte*, some English grammar, about which I can still learn all kinds of things, and finally, as the mood takes me, I write or read again. Then in the evening I am tired enough to be glad to lie down, though that does not mean going to sleep at once. . . .

22 October 1943[14]

I am told that Susanne has just been here with little Michael, to leave your parcel. Thank you, and her, very much for it. I hope the prison did not make too great an impression on the little boy; a child like that has as yet no standards by which to judge such things, and he may imagine that things are blacker for me than they are. I was really distressed not to be able to give him a friendly welcome and talk to him; it would certainly have reassured him. No doubt Susanne's point of view is that we ought not deliberately to keep children away from the experiences that life brings us; and I think that is right in principle. But when they are eighteen, how difficult they will be from what we were —not too disillusioned and bitter, I hope, but actually tougher and stronger because of all that they have been through. Please give Michael my best thanks for his bunch of flowers.

It seems as if my affairs are now beginning to move, and I am very glad of it; and it is the more anomalous that I cannot now, as I could formerly, discuss my concerns with you. But I don't think it can be very much

[14] The original of this letter is published in *Gesammelte Schriften* II, 442 f.

longer now. Anyway, you must not suppose that I am giving all my time to this business; that is not so at all, and I think there is no need for it. The last few days and weeks have been quiet, and I have been using them to do as much work as possible; unfortunately I never get through quite as much as I set out to during the day. I have had the great advantage of being able lately to read through undisturbed, and compare with each other, the great German educational and cultural novels, *Wilhelm Meister*, *Der Nachsommer*, *Der Grüne Heinrich*, *Der Hungerpastor* (at present I am on *Die Flegeljahre*), and I shall enjoy the recollection of them for a long time. I found it very useful, too, to read the *Weltgeschichte*. I still like Hartmann's *Systematische Philosophie* very much; it is a very handy survey. So I can feel as if I had been given a term at a university with a series of good lectures. Of course, any creative output of my own has suffered badly; but I am now looking forward tremendously to the day when I shall again be in touch, not only with ideas and fictitious figures, but with real people and all our many daily problems; it will be a very radical change.

Have you any news from Calabria[15] of Hans Christoph?[16] I am getting on all right, and am enjoying the last warm days of the year, as far as that is possible. Thank you very much for everything. I hope your anxiety will soon be over now; it is high time. . . .

31 October 1943

. . . Today is Reformation Day, a feast that in our time can give one plenty to think about. One wonders why Luther's action had to be followed by consequences that were the exact opposite of what he intended, and that darkened the last years of his life, so

---

[15] Referring to the war in Italy.

[16] Hans Christoph von Hase, a cousin nearly the same age as Bonhoeffer.

that he sometimes even doubted the value of his life's work. He wanted a real unity of the Church and the West—that is, of the Christian peoples, and the consequence was the disintegration of the Church and of Europe; he wanted the "freedom of the Christian man," and the consequence was indifference and licentiousness; he wanted the establishment of a genuine secular social order free from clerical privilege, and the result was insurrection, the Peasant's War, and soon afterwards the gradual dissolution of all real cohesion and order in society. I remember from my student days a discussion between Holl and Harnack as to whether the great historical intellectual and spiritual movements made headway through their primary or their secondary motives. At the time I thought Holl was right in maintaining the former; now I think he was wrong. As long as a hundred years ago Kirkegaard said that today Luther would say the opposite of what he said then. I think he was right—with some reservations.

Now another request. Would you please order for me *Lesebuch der Erzähler*, by Wolf Dietrich Rasch (Kiepenheuer, 1943), *Die Ballade*, by Wilhelm von Scholz (Theodor Knaur, 1943), and *Briefe der Liebe aus 8 Jahrhunderten*, by Friedrich Reck-Malleszewen (Keil, 1943)? There may not be a great number of copies printed, so they will have to be ordered at once.

A short time ago my rheumatism was so bad that for a few hours I could not get up from my chair without help, or even lift my hands to feed myself. But they at once gave me electrical treatment in the sick-bay, and it is much better now, though I have not been entirely free of it since May. Is there anything I can do about it later? . . .

9 November 1943

. . . I was very surprised and pleased with the Stifter anthology. As it consists mainly of extracts from his letters, it is almost all new to me. My overriding interest for the last ten days has been *Witiko*, which, after my giving you so much trouble to hunt for it, was discovered in the library here—a place where I should really not have expected it. Most people would find its thousand pages, which cannot be skipped but have to be taken steadily, too much for them, so I am not sure whether to recommend it to you. For me it is one of the finest books I know. The purity of its style and character-drawing gives one a quite rare and peculiar feeling of happiness. One really ought to read it for the first time at the age of fourteen, instead of the *Kampf um Rom*, and then grow up with it. Even the present-day good historical novels, e.g. those by Gertrud Bäumer, cannot compare with it—it is *sui generis*. I should very much like to have it, but it would hardly be possible to get hold of it. So far, the only historical novels that have made a comparable impression on me are *Don Quixote* and Gotthelf's *Berner Geist*. I have again failed to make anything of Jean Paul; I can't get over the feeling that he is vain and affected. He must have been rather unattractive personally, too. It is fine to go through literature like this on voyages of discovery, and one does discover some quite surprising things, even after so many years' reading. Perhaps you have further suggestions to make?

A few days ago I got R[üdiger]'s letter, for which I thank him very much. The programme of the Furt-wängler concert that he went to did make me wish I could have been there. I hope I shall not forget what is left of my technique while I am here. I sometimes feel a real craving for an evening of music—trio, quartet, or singing; one would like to hear something different from the voices in this building. After more than seven months here one has had more than enough of it. But of course, that is only to be expected, and

there is no need to mention it to you. What is not a
matter of course is that I am all right here in spite of
everything, that I can experience pleasures of one kind
or another, and that with it all I keep my spirits up—
and so I am very thankful every day. . . .

17 November 1943

While I am writing this letter, on Repentance Day,[17]
the S[chleicher]s are all listening to the Mass in B
Minor. For years now I have associated it with this
particular day, like the St. Matthew Passion with Good
Friday. I well remember the evening when I first heard
it. I was eighteen, and had just come from Harnack's
seminar, in which he had discussed my first seminar
essay very kindly, and had expressed the hope that
some day I should specialize in Church History. I was
full of this when I went into the Philharmonic Hall; the
great *Kyrie Eleison* was just beginning, and as it did
so, I forgot everything else—the effect was indescribable. Today I am going through it, bit by bit, in my
mind, and I am glad the S's can hear it, as it is my
favourite work of Bach. . . .

It is nearly evening now, and it is quiet in the building, so I can pursue my thoughts undisturbed. During
the day I keep on finding out again the different degrees
of noise with which people do their work; I suppose
that is how nature has endowed them. A *fortissimo*
just outside my cell is hardly the right background for
serious study.

I have very much enjoyed re-reading Goethe's *Rein-
ecke Fuchs* this last week. You might enjoy it again
too. . . .

---

[17] *Busstag*, the Wednesday before Remembrance Sunday
(*Totensonntag*; see p. 78).

The First Sunday in Advent,
28 November 1943

Although I don't know how letters are getting through at present, I want to write to you on the afternoon of the First Sunday in Advent. Altdorfer's "Nativity" is very topical this year, showing the Holy Family and the crib among the ruins of a tumbledown house. How ever did he come to paint like that, against all tradition, four hundred years ago? Perhaps he meant that Christmas could and should be kept even in such conditions; in any case, that is his message for us. I like to think of your sitting with the children and keeping Advent with them, just as you used to years ago with us. Only we do everything more intensively now, as we don't know how much longer we have.

It still makes me shudder to think what a distressing night you had, with one really bad moment, without any of us with you. It really is beyond me why I should be kept behind bars like this without being able to help in any way. I do hope it will soon be over now with no more delays. All the same, please don't worry about me. We shall come out of the whole business very much strengthened.

You will know already that we have had the expected attack on near-by Borsig. Now we have the (not very Christian) hope that they will not be coming round here again just yet. It was not exactly pleasant, and when I am released, I shall make some suggestions about improving the organization here for incidents of that kind. Most surprisingly, my window-panes were unbroken, whereas nearly all the others are smashed. It makes it horribly cold for the other people. As part of the prison wall has been wrecked, there can be no more "exercise" for the present. If only it were possible for us to hear from each other after the attacks! . . .

These last few days, I have been enjoying W. H. Riehl's *Geschichten aus alten Zeiten*. You may remember the book from a much earlier period. Today it is just about forgotten, though it is still very pleasant and enjoyable reading; it would also be suitable for reading aloud to the children. As far as I can remember, we had a few of his works at home, but we have probably given them away since then to some collection or other.

It would be very nice if you could bring me the book on superstition. They are starting to consult cards here about the chances of a raid during the coming night. It is interesting how superstition thrives in unsettled times, and how many are prepared to listen to it, at least with half an ear. . . .

17 December 1943

I am writing you a Christmas letter already, so as to be on the safe side. Although it passes my comprehension why they may possibly still keep me here over Christmas, I have learnt in the past eight and a half months that the unexpected often happens, and that what cannot be changed must be accepted with a *sacrificium intellectus*, although the *sacrificium* is not quite complete, and the *intellectus* silently goes its own way.

Above all, you must not think that I am going to let myself be depressed by this lonely Christmas; it will always take its special place among the other unusual Christmases that I have kept in Spain, America, and England, and I want in later years to look back on the time here, not with shame, but with a certain pride. That is the only thing that no one can take from me.

Of course, you . . . can't help thinking of my being in prison over Christmas, and it is bound to cast a shadow over the few happy hours that are left to you in these times. The only thing I can do to help is to believe and know that your thoughts about it will be the same as mine, and that we shall be as one in our attitude towards the keeping of the Christmas. Indeed, it cannot be otherwise, for that attitude is simply a spiritual inheritance from you. I need not tell you how I long to be released and to see you all again. But for years you have given us such perfectly lovely Christmases that our grateful recollection of them is strong enough to put a darker one into the background. It is not till such times as these that we realize what it means to possess a past and a spiritual inheritance independent of changes of time and circumstance. The consciousness of being borne up by a spiritual tradition that goes back for centuries gives one a feeling of confidence and security in the face of all passing strains and stresses. I believe that anyone who is aware of such reserves of strength need not be ashamed of more tender feelings evoked by the memory of a rich and noble past, for in my opinion they belong to the better and nobler part of mankind. They will not overwhelm those who hold fast to values that no one can take from them.

From the Christian point of view there is no special problem about Christmas in a prison cell. For many people in this building it will probably be a more sincere and genuine occasion than in places where nothing but the name is kept. That misery, suffering, poverty, loneliness, helplessness, and guilt mean something quite different in the eyes of God from what they mean in the judgment of man, that God will approach where men turn away, that Christ was born in a stable because there was no room for him in the inn—these are things that a prisoner can understand better than other people; for him they really are glad tidings, and that faith gives him a part in the communion of saints, a Christian fellowship breaking the bounds of time and space and reducing the months of confinement here to insignificance.

On Christmas Eve I shall be thinking of you all very much, and I want you to believe that I too shall have a few really happy hours, and that I am certainly not allowing my troubles to get the better of me. . . .

It is only when one thinks of the terrible times that so many people in Berlin have been through lately that one realizes how much we have to be thankful for. No doubt it will be a very quiet Christmas everywhere, and the children will remember it for a long time to come. But it may perhaps bring home to some people for the first time what Christmas really is. . . .

25 December 1943

Christmas is over. It brought me a few quiet, peaceful hours, and it revived a good many past memories. My gratitude for the preservation of yourselves and all the family in the heavy air raids, and my confidence that I shall see you again in the not too distant future, were greater than all my troubles. I lit the candles that you and M[aria] sent me, read the Christmas story and a few carols which I hummed over to myself; and in doing so, I thought of you all and hoped that, after all the alarms of the last few weeks, you might be able to enjoy an hour or two of peace. . . .

The New Year, too, will bring a great deal of anxiety and disturbance, though I think we may on this New Year's Eve sing with greater confidence than ever that verse from the old New Year's hymn:

> *Schleuss zu die Jammerpforten,*
> *und lass an allen Orten*
> *nach so viel Blutvergiessen*
> *die Freudenströme fliessen.*[18]

[18] Shut fast the doors of woe,
In every place let flow
The streams of joy and peace,
That bloodshed now may cease.

(Paul Gerhardt)

I know no greater prayer or wish than that. . . .

14 January 1944

. . . I am sitting by the open window, with the sunshine streaming in almost like spring, and I take this uncommonly fine start to the year for a good omen. Compared with last year, this year can only be better. —I am getting on all right. I am finding it a little easier to concentrate, and I am enjoying Dilthey very much. . . .

20 February 1944

Forgive me for not having written regularly lately. I had hoped to be able to give you some definite news about my case, so I put off writing from day to day. I was first assured quite definitely that the matter would be settled by July 1943; and then, as you will remember, it was to be September at the very latest. But now it is dragging on from month to month with nothing whatever happening. I am quite sure that if they only got down to business, the whole thing would be cleared up quite simply; and really, when one thinks of all the tasks waiting to be done outside, one is apt to feel, however hard one tries to be patient and understanding, that it is better to write no letters, but to say nothing for a time, first because disordered thoughts and feelings would only give rise to wrong words, and secondly because whatever one writes is likely to be quite out of date by the time it reaches its destination. Again and again it is something of an inward struggle to keep soberly to the facts, to banish illusions and fancies from my head, and to content myself with things as they are; for when one does not understand the external factors, one supposes that there must be some unseen internal factor at work. Besides, our generation cannot now lay claim to such a life as was possible in yours —a life that can find its full scope in professional and personal activities, and achieve balance and fulfillment. That is perhaps the greatest sacrifice that we younger people, with the example of your life still before our eyes, are called on and compelled to make, and it makes us particularly aware of the fragmentary and incomplete nature of our own. But this very fragmentariness may, in fact, point towards a fulfilment beyond the limits of human achievement; I have to keep that in mind, particularly in view of the death of so many of the best of my former pupils. Even if the pressure of outward events may split our lives into fragments, like bombs falling on houses, we must do our best to keep in view how the whole was planned and thought out; and we shall still be able to see what material was used, or was to be used, here for building. . . .

2 March 1944

. . . You probably heard from M[aria] that I told her last time (although we do not often mention the subject) that our meals here had become rather scantier because of reduced rations, and that I was sometimes rather hungry, though that was no doubt partly because I had hardly eaten anything during the few days when I had flu. Now once again you have looked after me nobly, and I must frankly admit that the world does sometimes have a different look if one has some good food inside one, and that the work goes better. All the same, I should hate to think I was depriving you of food when you have so much to do all day and need your strength more urgently than I do. Now March is here again, and still you have not been away for a holiday. . . .

I have been very impressed by Harnack's history of the Prussian Academy; it has made me feel both happy and unhappy. There are so few people now who want to have any intimate spiritual association with the eighteenth and nineteenth centuries: music tries to draw inspiration from the sixteenth and seventeenth centuries, theology from the time of the Reformation, philosophy from St. Thomas Aquinas and Aristotle, and the present *Weltanschauung* from bygone Teutonic days. But who bothers at all now about the work and achievements of our grandfathers, and how much of what they knew have we already forgotten? I believe that people will one day be quite amazed by what was achieved in that period, which is now so disregarded and so little known.

Could you please get hold of Dilthey's *Weltanschauung und Analyse des Menschen seit Renaissance und Reformation* for me? . . .

26 April 1944

This is my second spring in prison, but it is very different from last year's. Then all my impressions were fresh and vivid, and privations and pleasures were felt more keenly. Since then something has happened which I should never have thought possible—I have got used to things; and the only question is which has been greater, the growth of insensitivity or the clarification of experience—it probably varies in different connections. The things towards which we become insensitive are soon forgotten, as they are of no great consequence; but there are other things, which we have consciously or unconsciously assimilated and cannot forget. Intense experience forges them into convictions, resolutions, and plans, and as such they are important for our lives in the future. It certainly makes a great difference whether one is in prison for a month or a year; in the latter case one absorbs not only an interesting or intense impression, but a radically new kind of life. At the same time I think that certain inward preconditions are necessary to enable one to assimilate this particular aspect of life without danger, and I think a long imprisonment is extremely dangerous for very young people as far as their spiritual development is concerned. The impressions come with such violence that they may well sweep a great deal overboard.

I must thank you very much for the way you are continually making things easier for me by your regular visits, letters, and parcels. The great joy that your greetings give me has remained constant from the first, and always encourages me afresh to use my time here to the full. . . . I wonder whether you could try to get me Ortega y Gasset's new book, *The Nature of Historical Crises*, and, if possible, his earlier work, *History as a System*, and also H. Pfeffer's *Das britische Empire und die U.S.A.* I hope we shall meet again soon.

> With much love,
> Your grateful
> Dietrich.

5

REPORT ON PRISON LIFE

THE FORMALITIES OF admission were correctly completed. For the first night I was locked up in an admission cell. The blankets on the camp bed had such a foul smell that in spite of the cold it was impossible to use them. Next morning a piece of bread was thrown into my cell; I had to pick it up from the floor. A quarter of the coffee consisted of grounds. The sound of the prison staff's vile abuse of the prisoners who were held for investigation penetrated into my cell for the first time; since then I have heard it every day from morning till night. When I had to parade with the other new arrivals, we were addressed by one of the jailers as "blackguards," etc. etc. We were all asked why we had been arrested, and when I said I did not know, the jailer answered with a scornful laugh, "You'll find that out soon enough." It was six months before I got a warrant for my arrest. As we went through the various offices, some NCOs, who had heard what my profession was, wanted now and then to have a few words with me. They were told that no one was to talk to me. While I was having a bath an NCO (I do not know who he was) suddenly appeared and asked me whether I knew Pastor N.[1] When I said that I did, he

[1] Martin Niemöller.

exclaimed, "He is a good friend of mine," and disappeared again. I was taken to the most isolated single cell on the top floor; a notice, prohibiting all access without special permission, was put outside it. I was told that all my correspondence would be stopped until further notice, and that, unlike all the other prisoners, I should not be allowed half an hour a day in the open air, although, according to the prison rules, I was entitled to it. I received neither newspapers nor anything to smoke. After 48 hours my Bible was returned to me; it had been searched to see whether I had smuggled inside it a saw, razor blades, or the like. For the next twelve days the cell door was opened only for bringing food in and putting the bucket out. No one said a word to me. I was told nothing about the reason for my detention, or how long it would last. I gathered from various remarks—and it was confirmed later— that I was lodged in the section for the most serious cases, where the condemned prisoners lay shackled.

The first night in my cell I could not sleep much, because in the next cell a prisoner wept loudly for several hours on end; no one took any notice. I thought at the time that that kind of thing would happen every night, but in all the months since then it has only been repeated once. In those first days of complete isolation I could see nothing of how things were run in the building; I could only picture what was going on from the incessant shouting of the warders. My basic impression, which is still unchanged, was that anyone detained for investigation was at once treated as a criminal, and that in practice it was impossible for a prisoner who was treated unjustly to get redress. Later I more than once heard conversations in which warders said quite bluntly that if a prisoner complained of unjust treatment, or of being struck (which is strictly forbidden), the authorities would never believe the prisoner, but always the warder, especially as the latter could be sure of finding a colleague who would testify for him on oath. I have, in fact, known of cases where this evil practice was followed.

After twelve days the authorities got to know of my family connections. While this was a great relief to me personally, it was most embarrassing to see how everything changed from that moment. I was put into a more spacious cell, which one of the men cleaned every day for me; I was offered larger rations, which I always refused, as they would have been at the expense of the other prisoners; the captain fetched me for a daily walk, with the result that the staff treated me with studied politeness—in fact, several of them came to apologize: "We didn't know," etc. It was painful.

General treatment: The tone is set by those warders who behave in the most evil and brutal way towards the prisoners. The whole building resounds with vile and insulting abuse, so that the quieter and more fair-minded warders, too, are nauseated by it, but they can hardly exercise any influence. During months of detention for investigation, prisoners who are later acquitted have to suffer abuse like criminals, and are absolutely defenceless, since their right to complain exists only in theory. Private means, cigarettes, and promises for later on play an important part. The little man with no connections etc. has to submit to everything. The same people who rant and rage at the other prisoners show a servile politeness towards me. Attempts to have a quiet word with them about the treatment of all the other prisoners fail because, although they admit everything at the time, they are just as bad as ever an hour later. I must not omit to say that a number of the warders are even-tempered, matter-of-fact, and, as far as possible, friendly towards the prisoners; but they mostly remain in subordinate posts.

Food: Prisoners cannot avoid the impression that they do not receive in full the rations due to them.

There is often not the slightest trace of the meat that is alleged to be included in the soup. Bread and sausage are divided very unequally. I weighed one sausage ration myself; it was 15 grammes instead of 25. NCOs and others working in the kitchen have plenty of unhappy impressions and observations about this. With 700 prisoners to be fed, even the smallest inaccuracy makes a big difference. I know for a fact that when the doctors or officers inspect the prisoners' food, a nourishing sauce made of meat or cream is added to the plates concerned; and so it is not surprising that the prisoners' food has a high reputation. I also know that the meat intended for the prisoners has all the goodness boiled out of it first in the cauldrons where the staff's food is cooked, and so on. An occasional comparison between the prisoners' food and the staff's is simply staggering. On Sundays and holidays the food is not examined, and the midday meal is beneath all criticism; it consists of cabbage soup made with water and with no fat, meat, or potatoes at all. It seems to me beyond doubt that the food provided is quite inadequate for young people detained for any length of time. No records are kept of the prisoners' weight. Although these prisoners are only being held for investigation, and are, moreover, soldiers, some of whom are sent straight back to their units when they are released, they are told that they are strictly forbidden, on pain of severe punishment, to receive food parcels. No articles of food are allowed in—not even the eggs and sandwiches that the prisoners' relatives bring them on visiting days. This causes great bitterness among the prisoners and their visitors. Military police who deliver the prisoners are looked after—against standing orders—in the kitchen.

Occupation: By far the greater part of the prisoners detained for investigation spend the day without any work, although most of them ask for work. They receive three books a week from a very mediocre library. Games of every kind, such as chess, are forbidden, even in the communal cells, and if any of the prisoners have managed to make themselves one, it is taken away from them and they are punished. There are no projects for work that would be useful for all the 700 prisoners, such as, for instance, the construction of air raid shelters. There are no religious services. The prisoners, some of whom are very young (they include anti-aircraft auxiliaries)[2] are bound to suffer in body and soul from the lack of occupation and of supervision, particularly during a long, solitary confinement.

Lighting: During the winter months the prisoners often had to sit in the dark for several hours because the staff were too lazy to switch on the cell lights. When the prisoners, who have a right to lighting in their cells, put out their flags or knocked to get attention, the staff would shout angrily at them, and the light would not be switched on till the next day. The prisoners are not allowed to lie on their beds before the Last Post, so that they had to spend the hours before that sitting in the dark. That is very depressing, and only causes bitterness.

Air raid warnings: There are no air raid shelters for the prisoners. With all the labour available here, it would have been quite easy to provide these in good time. A dug-out has been built, but only for the authorities; apart from that, all that happens is that the prisoners on the top floor are locked in with the others in the ground-floor cells. When I asked why the prisoners in the second-floor cells were not moved down to the first floor, I was told that it would make too much work. There is no first-aid shelter. When the sick-bay was put out of action during a heavy attack, they could not start to bandage the injured till after it was over. No one who has experienced it will ever forget the

[2] Anti-aircraft auxiliaries (*Flakhelfer*) were between fifteen and seventeen years of age.

shouting and screaming of the locked-up prisoners during a heavy air-raid—some of them are here because of trifling offences, or are actually innocent. Seven hundred soldiers are exposed here to the dangers of a bombing attack with no protection.

Miscellaneous: The only way in which a prisoner can communicate with the staff in case of urgency is by putting out the flag. This is often ignored for hours, or perhaps a passing warder simply pushes it back without finding out what the prisoner wants. If the prisoner then knocks on the door, he gets a volley of abuse. If he reports sick outside the regulation hours, he inconveniences the staff, and is therefore in most cases angrily shouted at; it is only with great difficulty that he manages to gain access to the sick-bay. I have twice known prisoners to be kicked into it; one of them had acute appendicitis and had to be taken to the military hospital at once, and the other was suffering from prolonged hysterical convulsions.—All those who are detained for investigation, even for the most minor offences, appear in chains at their interrogation and trial. This is a great humiliation for a soldier in uniform, and makes the interrogation a more severe ordeal for him.—The men who empty the buckets and bring round the food receive the same small amount of soap for washing as the ordinary prisoners, and even for the latter it is hardly enough.

6

LETTERS TO A FRIEND,[1]
POEMS AND MISCELLANEOUS PAPERS

18 November 1943

As YOU ARE in the neighbourhood, I simply must take the opportunity of writing to you. I expect you know that I have not even been allowed to have a clergyman to see me here. . . . So let me tell you a little that you ought to know about me. For the first twelve days, during which I was segregated and treated as a felon—up to now the cells on each side of me have been occupied almost solely by handcuffed men awaiting death—Paul Gerhardt has been an unexpectedly helpful standby, and so have the Psalms and Revelation. During this time I have been preserved from any serious spiritual trial. You are the only person who knows how often *accidie, tristitia*, with all its menacing consequences, have lain in wait for me; and I feared at the time that you must be worrying about me on that account. But I told myself from the beginning that I was not going to oblige either man or devil in any such way—they can do what they like about it for themselves; and I hope I shall always be able to stand firm on this.—At first I wondered a good deal whether it was really for the cause of Christ that I was causing you all such grief; but I soon put that out of my head as a temptation, as

[1] Eberhard Bethge.

69

I became certain that the duty had been laid on me to hold out in this boundary situation with all its problems; I became quite content to do this, and have remained so ever since (I Peter 2.20; 3.14).

I have reproached myself for not having finished my *Ethics* (parts of it have probably been confiscated), and it was some consolation to me that I had told you the essentials, and that even if you had forgotten it, it would probably emerge again indirectly somehow. Besides, my ideas were still incomplete.

I also felt it to be an omission not to have carried out my long-cherished wish to attend the Lord's Supper once again with you . . ., and yet I know that we have shared spiritually, although not physically, in the gift of confession, absolution, and communion, and that we may be quite happy and easy in our minds about it. But I did just want to tell you this.

As soon as it was possible, apart from my daily work on the Bible (I have read through the Old Testament two and a half times and learnt a great deal), I began to do some non-theological work. An essay on "The feeling of time" originated mainly in the need to bring before me my own past in a situation that could so easily seem "empty" and "wasted." Our past is always kept before us by thankfulness and penitence. But more of that later.

Then I started on a bold enterprise that I have had in mind for a long time: I began to write the story of a contemporary middle-class family. The background for this consisted of all our innumerable conversations on the subject, and my own personal experiences; in short, it was to present afresh middle-class life as we know it in our own families, and especially in the light of Christianity. It tells of two families on terms of friendship living in a small town. Their children grow up, and as they gradually enter into the responsibilities of official positions, they try to work together for the good of the community as mayor, teacher, pastor, doctor, engineer. You would recognize many familiar features, and you come into it too. But I have not yet got much further than the beginning, mainly because the repeated false forecasts of my release have made it difficult for me to concentrate. But the work is giving me great pleasure. Only I wish I could talk it over with you every day; indeed, I miss that more than you think. . . .

Incidentally, I have written an essay on "What is 'speaking the truth?' ", and at the moment I am trying to write some prayers for prisoners; it is surprising that there are none, and perhaps these may be distributed at Christmas.

And now for my reading. Yes, E., I am very sorry that we did not get to know Stifter together; it would have helped us very much in our talks, but we shall have to put it off till later. But I have a great deal to tell you about that. Later? When and how will it come about? To be on the safe side, I have made my will and given it to my lawyer. . . . But you are almost certain to be in greater danger than I am. I shall be thinking of you every day and asking God to bring you back safely. . . . I wonder whether, if I am not condemned, but released and called up, it might be arranged for me to join your regiment. That would be fine! Anyway, if I should be condemned (one never knows), don't worry about me. It really does not worry me at all, except that in that case I shall probably be kept here for a few more months longer "on probation,"[2] and that is really not pleasant. But there is a great deal that is not pleasant! The thing for which I should be condemned is so unexceptionable that I should only be proud of it. But I hope that, if God preserves us, we shall at least be able to celebrate Easter happily together. . . .

[2] A veiled expression of hope that Hitler would soon be overthrown.

But let us promise to remain faithful in interceding for each other. I shall ask that you may have strength, health, patience, and protection from conflicts and temptations. You can ask for the same things for me. And if it should be decided that we are not to meet again, let us remember each other to the end in thankfulness and forgiveness, and may God grant us that one day we may stand before his throne praying for each other and joining in praise and thankfulness.

. . . I am finding here (I expect you are, too) that the most difficult thing is getting up in the morning (Jer. 31.26!). I am now praying quite simply for freedom. There is such a thing as a false composure which is quite unchristian. As Christians, we need not be at all ashamed of some impatience, longing, opposition to what is unnatural, and our full share of desire for freedom, earthly happiness, and opportunity for effective work. I think we entirely agree about that.

Well, in spite of everything, or rather because of everything, that we are now going through, each in his own way, we shall still be the same as before, shan't we? I hope you don't think I am here turning out to be a "man of the inner line";[3] I was never in less danger of that, and I think the same applies to you. What a happy day it will be when we tell each other our experiences. But I sometimes get very angry at not being free yet! . . .

PRAYERS FOR FELLOW-PRISONERS

Christmas 1943

MORNING PRAYERS

O God, early in the morning I cry to thee.
Help me to pray

[3] The *Männer der inneren Linie'* (the *"Bund der Mitte"*) were churchmen who disliked Hitler's anti-Christian dictatorship, but who, under pressure, abandoned their opposition to it.

And to concentrate my thoughts on thee;
I cannot do this alone.

In me there is darkness,
But with thee there is light;
I am lonely, but thou leavest me not;
I am feeble in heart, but with thee there is help;
I am restless, but with thee there is peace.
In me there is bitterness, but with thee there is patience;
I do not understand thy ways,
But thou knowest the way for me.

O heavenly Father,
I praise and thank thee
For the peace of the night;
I praise and thank thee for this new day;
I praise and thank thee for all thy goodness
and faithfulness throughout my life.

Thou hast granted me many blessings;
Now let me also accept what is hard
from thy hand.
Thou wilt lay on me no more
than I can bear.
Thou makest all things work together for good
for thy children.

Lord Jesus Christ,
Thou wast poor
and in distress, a captive and forsaken as I am.
Thou knowest all man's troubles;
Thou abidest with me
when all men fail me;
Thou rememberest and seekest me;
It is thy will that I should know thee
and turn to thee.
Lord, I hear thy call and follow;
Do thou help me.

O Holy Spirit,
Give me faith that will protect me
from despair, from passions, and from vice;
Give me such love for God and men

as will blot out all hatred and bitterness;
Give me the hope that will deliver me
from fear and faint-heartedness.

O holy and merciful God,
my Creator and Redeemer,
my Judge and Saviour,
Thou knowest me and all that I do.
Thou dost hate and punish evil without respect of persons
in this world and the next;
Thou forgivest the sins of those
who sincerely pray for forgiveness;
Thou lovest goodness, and rewardest it on this earth
with a clear conscience,
and, in the world to come,
with a crown of righteousness.

I remember in thy presence all my loved ones,
my fellow-prisoners, and all who in this house
perform their hard service;
Lord, have mercy.
Restore me to liberty,
and enable me so to live now
that I may answer before thee and before men.
Lord, whatever this day may bring,
Thy name be praised.
Amen.

Wenn ich schlafe, wacht sein Sorgen
und ermuntert mein Gemüt,
da ich alle liebe Morgen
schaue neue Lieb' und Güt'.
Wäre mein Gott nicht gewesen,
hätte mich sein Angesicht
nicht geleitet, wär' ich nicht
aus so mancher Angst genesen.
Alles Ding währt seine Zeit,
Gottes Lieb' in Ewigkeit.[4]

(Paul Gerhardt)

[4] "While I sleep, he watches over me and refreshes my spirit,
and his lovingkindness is new every morning. If God had not

EVENING PRAYERS

O Lord my God, I thank thee
that thou has brought this day to a close;
I thank thee for giving me rest
in body and soul.
Thy hand has been over me
and has guarded and preserved me.
Forgive my lack of faith
and any wrong that I have done today,
and help me to forgive all who have wronged me.

Let me sleep in peace under thy protection,
and keep me from all the temptations of darkness.

Into thy hands I commend my loved ones
and all who dwell in this house;
I commend to thee my body and soul.
O God, thy holy name be praised.
Amen.

Ein Tag, der sagt dem andern,
mein Leben sei ein Wandern
zur grossen Ewigkeit.
O Ewigkeit, so schöne,
mein Herz an dich gewöhne;
mein Heim ist nicht in dieser Zeit.[5]

(Gerhard Tersteegen)

---

been with me and led me by the light of his countenance, my
anxieties would have prevailed over me. Everything has its
day, but God's love is eternal."

[5] "Each day tells the next that my life is a journey to eternity. O great and beautiful eternity, attune my heart to thee,
for this present time is not my home."

PRAYERS IN TIME OF DISTRESS

O Lord God,
great distress has come upon me;
my cares threaten to crush me,
and I do not know what to do.
O God, be gracious to me and help me.
Give me strength to bear what thou dost send,
and do not let fear rule over me;
Take a father's care of my wife and children.

O merciful God,
forgive me all the sins that I have committed
against thee and against my fellow men.
I trust in thy grace
and commit my life wholly into thy hands.
Do with me according to thy will
and as is best for me.
Whether I live or die, I am with thee,
and thou, my God, art with me.
Lord, I wait for thy salvation
and for thy kingdom.
Amen.

Unverzagt und ohne Grauen
soll ein Christ, wo er ist,
stets sich lassen schauen.
Wollt' ihn auch der Tod aufreiben,
soll der Mut dennoch gut
und fein stille bleiben.
Kann uns doch kein Tod nicht töten,
sondern reisst unsern Geist
aus viel tausend Nöten,
Schliest das Tor der bittern Leiden
und macht Bahn, da man kann
gehn zu Himmelsfreuden.[6]

(Paul Gerhardt)

[6] "A Christian should constantly show you where he is, fearless and undismayed. Even though death itself should assail
him, let him be calm and of good courage. For death cannot

LETTERS TO A FRIEND

20 November 1943

. . . If I should still be kept in this hole over Christmas, don't worry about it. I am not really anxious about it. One can keep Christmas as a Christian even in prison—more easily than family occasions, anyhow. Thank you especially for applying for permission to visit me; I don't expect, either, that there have been any complications this time. I certainly should not have ventured to ask you to do anything about it; but as you yourself have made the move, it is much better. I really do hope it comes off. But, you know, even if it is refused, we shall still be glad that you tried, and it will only make us rather more angry with certain people[7] for the time being—and there is no harm in that (indeed, I sometimes think I am not yet angry enough about the whole business!). So in that case we will swallow even that bitter pill, for after all, we have both of us been getting used to that kind of thing lately. I am glad I saw you just as I was arrested, and I shall not forget it. . . .

A little more about my daily routine: We get up at the same time, and the day lasts till 8 p.m.; I wear out my trousers by sitting while you wear out your soles by walking. I read the *Völkischer Beobachter* and the *Reich*, and I have gotten to know several *very* nice people. Every day I am taken for half an hour's walking alone, and in the afternoon they give me treatment in the sick-bay—very kindly, but unsuccessfully—for my rheumatism. Every week I get from you the most marvellous things to eat. Thank you very much for everything, and

---

kill us; it can but snatch our spirit away from much distress, shut the door of bitter sorrows, and open the way by which we can enter into the joys of heaven."

[7] Dr. Roeder, who led the prosecution.

also for the cigars and cigarettes that you sent me while you were away. I only hope you have plenty to eat— do you get very hungry? That would be horrid. There is nothing I miss here—except all of you. I wish I could play the G minor sonata with you and sing some Schütz, and hear you sing Psalms 70 and 47; that was what you did best.

My cell is being cleaned out for me, and while it is being done, I can give the cleaner something to eat. One of them was sentenced to death the other day; it gave me a great shock.—One sees a great deal in seven and a half months, particularly what heavy conse- quences may follow trivial acts of folly. I think a lengthy confinement is demoralizing in *every* way for most people. I have been thinking out an alternative penal system on the principle of making the punishment fit the crime; e.g., for absence without leave, the can- celling of leave; for unauthorized wearing of medals, longer service at the front; for robbing other soldiers, the temporary labelling of a man as a thief; for dealing in the black market, a reduction of rations; and so on. Why does the Old Testament law never punish anyone by depriving him of his freedom?

21 November 1943

Today is Remembrance Sunday . . . and after it comes Advent, with all its happy memories for us. . . . Life in a prison cell may well be compared to Advent; one waits, hopes, and does this, that, or the other—things that are really of no consequence—the door is shut, and can be opened only *from the outside*. That idea is just as it occurs to me; don't suppose we go in very much for symbolism here! But I must tell you two other things that may surprise you: First, I very much miss meal-time fellowship. Everything that I get from you for my material enjoyment becomes here a reminder of my table-fellowship with you. So may not this be an essential part of life, because it is a reality of the Kingdom of God? Secondly, I have found that following Luther's instruction to "make the sign of the cross" at our morning and evening prayers is in itself helpful. There is something objective about it, and that is what is particularly badly needed here. Don't be alarmed; I shall not come out of here a *homo religiosus*! On the contrary, my fear and distrust of "religiosity" have become greater than ever here. The fact that the Israelites *never* uttered the name of God always makes me think, and I can understand it better as I go on.

. . . I am now reading Tertullian, Cyprian, and others of the Church Fathers with great interest. In some ways they are more relevant to our time than the Reformers, and at the same time they provide a basis for talks between Protestants and Roman Catholics.

. . . For the rest, I believe that on purely legal grounds my condemnation is out of the question.

22 November 1943

. . . Just tell me how you get on with the soldiers, with your willingness to take no notice of false accusations . . . Two or three times here I have given people a quite colossal dressing down for indulging in only the slightest rudeness, and they were so disconcerted that they have behaved very correctly since then. I thoroughly enjoy this sort of thing, but I know it is really an impossible over-sensitiveness that I can hardly get rid of. . . . It makes me furious to see quite defenceless people being unjustly shouted at and insulted. These petty tormentors, who can rage like that and whom one finds everywhere, get me worked up for hours on end.

. . . *Das Neue Lied*, which I got only a few days ago, has brought back hosts of pleasant memories. You see, I am always thinking of things that I want to talk over with you, and when I start again after such a long time, I find it difficult to stop. . . .

23 November 1943

Tonight's raid was not exactly pleasant. I kept on thinking . . . about you all. At such times prison life is no joke. I hope you are going back to S.[8] I was surprised last night to see how nervy the soldiers who had been at the front were while the alarm was on. . . .

24 November 1943

After yesterday's air raid I think it is only right that I should tell you briefly what arrangements I have made in case of my death. . . . I hope you will read this with your usual absence of sentimentality. . . .

Friday, 26 November 1943

So it really came off! Only for a moment, but that does not matter so much; even a few hours would be far too little, and when we are isolated here we can take in so much that even a few minutes gives us something to think about for a long time afterwards. It will be with me for a long time now—the memory of having the four people who are nearest and dearest to me with me for a brief moment. When I got back to my cell afterwards, I paced up and down for a whole hour, while my dinner stood there and got cold, so that at last I could not help laughing at myself when I found myself repeating over and over again, "That was really great!" I always hesitate to use the word "indescribable" about anything, because if you take enough trouble to make a thing clear, I think there is very little that is really "indescribable"—but at the moment that

---

[8] Sakrow, a village near Potsdam, where the Dohnanyis lived.

is just what this morning seems to be. Karl [Barth]'s
cigar is on the table in front of me, and that is something really indescribable—it was so kind and thought-
ful of him, and V.[9] too. How grand it was that you
saw them. And the good old favourite "Wolf" cigar
from Hamburg, which I used to be so fond of in better
times. Just by me, standing on a box, is the Advent
wreath, and on the shelf there are (among other things)
your gigantic eggs, waiting for breakfasts still to come.
(It is no use my saying that you ought not to have
deprived yourselves of them; but that is what I think,
though I am glad of them all the same). . . . I can
remember that my first visit to a prison (I went to see
Fritz Onnasch, and you were with me) took it out of
me terribly, although Fritz was very cheerful and nice.
I hope you did not feel like that when you were here
today. You see, it would be wrong to suppose that
prison life is uninterrupted torture. It certainly is not,
and visits like yours relieve it for days on end, even
though they do, of course, awaken feelings that have
fortunately lain dormant for a while. But that does not
matter either. I realize again in thankfulness how well
off I was, and feel new hope and energy. Thank you
very much, you yourself and all the others. . . .

27 November 1943

. . . Meanwhile we have had the expected large-scale
attack on Borsig. It really is a strange feeling, to see the
"Christmas trees," the flares that the leading aircraft
drops, coming down right over our heads. The shouting and screaming of the prisoners in their cells was
terrible. We had no dead, only injured, and we had
finished bandaging them by one o'clock. After that, I
was able to drop off at once into a sound sleep. People
here talk quite openly about how frightened they were.
I don't quite know what to make of it, for fright is

[9] Visser 't Hooft.

surely something to be ashamed of. I have a feeling
that it should not be talked about except in the confessional, otherwise it might easily involve a certain
amount of exhibitionism; and *a fortiori* there is no
need to play the hero. On the other hand, naïve frankness can be quite disarming. But even so, there is a
cynical, I might almost say ungodly, frankness, the
kind that breaks out in heavy drinking and fornication,
and gives the impression of chaos. I wonder whether
fright is not one of the *pudenda*, which ought to be concealed; I must think about it further; you have no doubt
formed your own ideas on the subject.

The fact that the horrors of war are now coming
home to us with such force will no doubt, if we survive,
provide us with the necessary basis for making it possible to reconstruct the life of the nations, both spiritually
and materially, on Christian principles. So we must try
to keep these experiences in our minds, use them in
our work, make them bear fruit, and not just shake
them off. Never have we been so plainly conscious of
the wrath of God, and that is a sign of his grace: "O
that today you would hearken to his voice! Harden not
your hearts" (Ps. 95.7f.). The tasks that confront us
are immense, but we must prepare ourselves for them
now and be ready when they come.

28 November 1943

The first Sunday in Advent.—It began with a peaceful
night. When I was in bed yesterday evening I looked
up for the first time "our" Advent hymns in the *Neues
Lied*. I can hardly hum any of them to myself without
being reminded of Finkenwalde, Schlönwitz, and Sigurdshof.[10] Early this morning I held my Sunday service, hung up the Advent wreath on a nail, and fastened
Lippi's picture of the Nativity in the middle of it. At

[10] Preachers' seminaries set up by the Confessing Church in
Pomerania.

breakfast I greatly enjoyed the second of your ostrich eggs. Soon after that, I was taken to the sick-bay for an interview which lasted till noon. The last air raid brought some most unpleasant experiences—a land-mine 25 yards away; a sick-bay with no lights or windows, prisoners screaming for help, with no one but ourselves taking any notice of them; but we too could do very little to help in the darkness, and one has to be cautious about opening the cell doors of those with the heaviest sentences, for you never know whether they will hit you on the head with a chair leg and try to get away. In short, it was not very nice. As a result, I wrote a report[11] of what had taken place, pointing out the need of medical attention during air raids. I hope it will be of some use. I am glad to be able to help in any way with reasonable suggestions.

By the way, I forgot to tell you that I smoked the fabulously fragrant "Wolf" cigar yesterday afternoon during a pleasant conversation in the sick-bay. Thank you very much for it. Since the raids started, the cigarette situation has unfortunately become calamitous. While the injured people were being bandaged, they asked for a cigarette, and the medical orderlies and I had already used up a lot beforehand; so I am all the more grateful for what you brought me the day before yesterday. Nearly every window in the place has been blown out, and the men are sitting in their cells freezing. Although I had forgotten to open my windows when I left the cell, I found at night to my great surprise that they were undamaged. I am very glad about that, although I am terribly sorry for the others.

How good it is that you can be at home to celebrate Advent. Just now you will be singing the first hymns together. It makes me think of Altdorfer's "Nativity" and the verse

[11] See p. 63.

Die Krippe glänzt hell und klar,
die Nacht gibt ein neu Licht dar,
Dunkel muss nicht kommen drein,
der Glaub bleibt immer im Schein.[12]—

and also the Advent melody

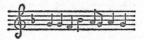

though not in four-four time, but in a flowing expectant rhythm to suit the text. After this I am going to read another of W. H. Riehl's entertaining stories. You would enjoy them, too, and they would do very well for reading aloud to the family. You must try to get hold of them some time.

29 November 1943

Today is quite different from all the previous Mondays. Usually on Monday mornings the shouting and swearing in the corridors is at its fiercest, but after the experiences of last week even the loudest shouters and bullies have become quite subdued—a most obvious change. Now there's something I must tell you personally: the heavy air raids, especially the last one, when the windows of the sick-bay were blown out by the land mine, and bottles and medical supplies fell down from the cupboards and shelves, and I lay on the floor in the darkness with little hope of coming through the attack safely, led me back quite simply to prayer and the Bible. More about that later when I see you. In more than one respect my time of imprisonment is being a very wholesome though drastic cure. But the details must wait till I can tell you personally.

---

[12] "The crib gleams bright and clear, the night brings a new light: darkness must not come within, faith always remains in light."

30 November 1943

Roeder[13] was too anxious at first to finish me for good; but he has now to content himself with a most ridiculous charge, which will bring him little glory. . . .

In the months that have passed I have learnt as never before that I owe all the alleviations and help that I get here, not to myself, but to others. . . . The wish to be independent in everything is false pride. Even what we owe to others belongs to ourselves and is a part of our own lives, and any attempt to calculate what we have "earned" for ourselves and what we owe to other people is certainly not Christian, and is, moreover, a futile undertaking. It is through what he himself is, plus what he receives, that a man becomes a complete entity. I wanted to tell you this, because I have now experienced it for myself, though not for the first time, for it was already implicit all through the years of our *vita communis*.

Advent II

I so much want to spend a quiet Sunday morning talking things over with you, and I am so tempted by the thought that a letter like this might help you to pass a quiet solitary hour, that I will write to you, though I don't know whether, or how, or where this will reach you. . . . How and where will the two of us be keeping Christmas this time? I hope you will manage to communicate something of its joy . . . to your fellow-soldiers. For the calmness and joy with which we meet what is laid on us are as infectious as the terror that I see among the people here at each new attack. Indeed, I think such an attitude gives one the greatest authority, provided that it is genuine and natural, and not merely for show. People need some constant factor to guide them. We are neither of us daredevils, but that has

13 See p. 77, n. 2.

nothing to do with the courage that comes from the grace of God.

My thoughts and feelings seem to be getting more and more like those of the Old Testament, and in recent months I have been reading the Old Testament much more than the New. It is only when one knows the unutterability of the name of God that one can utter the name of Jesus Christ; it is only when one loves life and the earth so much that without them everything seems to be over that one can believe in the resurrection and a new world; it is only when one submits to God's law that one can speak of grace; and it is only when God's wrath and vengeance are hanging as grim realities over the heads of one's enemies that something of what it means to love and forgive them can touch our hearts. In my opinion it is not Christian to want to take our thoughts and feelings too quickly and too directly from the New Testament. We have already talked about this several times, and every day confirms my opinion. One cannot and must not speak the last word before the last but one. We live in the last but one and believe the last, don't we? Lutherans (so-called!) and pietists would shudder at the thought, but it is true all the same. In *The Cost of Discipleship* (ch. 1) I just hinted at this, but did not follow it up; I must do so later. But the logical conclusions are far-reaching, e.g. for the problem of Catholicism, for the concept of the ministry, for the use of the Bible, etc., and above all for ethics. Why is it that in the Old Testament men tell lies vigorously and often to the glory of God (I have now collected the passages), kill, deceive, rob, divorce, and even fornicate (see the genealogy of Jesus), doubt, blaspheme, and curse, whereas in the New Testament there is nothing of all this? "An earlier stage" of religion? That is a very naïve way out; it is one and the same God. But more of this later when we meet.

Meanwhile evening has come. The NCO who has

just brought me from the sick-bay to my quarters said to me as he left, with an embarrassed smile but quite seriously, "Pray for us, Padre, that we may have no alarm tonight."

For some time I have been taking my daily walk with a man who has been a District Orator, Regional Leader, Government Director, former member of the governing body of the German-Christian Church in Brunswick, and is at present a Party Leader in Warsaw. He has completely gone to pieces here, and clings to me just like a child, consulting me about every little thing, telling me whenever he has cried, etc. After being very cool with him for several weeks, I am now able to ease things for him a little; his gratitude is quite touching, and he tells me again and again how glad he is to have met a man like me here. Well, the strangest situations do come about; if only I could tell you properly about them!

I have been thinking again over what I wrote to you recently about our own fear. I think that here, under the guise of honesty, something is being passed off as "natural" that is at bottom a symptom of sin; it is really quite analogous to talking openly about sexual matters. After all, "truthfulness" does not mean uncovering everything that exists. God himself made clothes for men; and that means that *in statu corruptionis* many things in human life ought to remain covered, and that evil, even though it cannot be eradicated, ought at least to be covered. Exposure is cynical, and although the cynic prides himself on his exceptional honesty, or claims to want truth at all costs, he misses the crucial fact that since the fall there must be reticence and secrecy. In my opinion the greatness of Stifter lies in his refusal to force his way into man's inner life, in his respect for reticence, and in his willingness to observe people more or less cautiously from the outside but not from the inside. Inquisitiveness is alien to him. I remember once

being impressed when Frau von K. told me with genuine horror about a film that showed the growth of a
plant speeded up; she said that she and her husband
could not stand it, as they felt it to be an impermissible
prying into the mystery of life. Stifter takes a similar
line. But is not this somewhat akin to the so-called
English "hypocrisy," which we contrast with German
"honesty?" I believe we Germans have never properly
grasped the meaning of "concealment," i.e. what is in
the end the *status corruptionis* of the world. Kant says
quite rightly in his *Anthropologie* that anyone who mis-
understands or questions the significance of outward
appearance in the world is a traitor to humanity.

By the way, was it you who got hold of the *Witiko*
that was brought to me on Friday? Who else could it
have been? Although it is painstaking rather than bril-
liant, I found parts of it very interesting. Thank you
very much.

"Speaking the truth" (on which I have written an
essay) means, in my opinion, saying how something
really is—that is, showing respect for secrecy, intimacy,
and concealment. "Betrayal," for example, is not truth,
any more than are flippancy, cynicism, etc. What is
secret may be revealed only in confession, i.e. in the
presence of God. More about that later, too.

There are two ways of dealing psychically with ad-
versities. One way, the easier, is to try to ignore them;
that is about as far as I have gotten. The other and more
difficult way is to face them deliberately and overcome
them; I am not equal to that yet, but one must learn to
do it, for the first way is a slight, though, I believe, a
permissible, piece of self-deception.

15 December 1943

When I read your letter yesterday, I felt as though a
spring, without which my intellectual life was beginning to dry up, had begun once again to produce the

first drops of water for a long, long time. Of course, that may sound to you an exaggeration ... but in my isolation, it is nothing of the kind. I am forced to live on the past. .... In any case, your letter set my thoughts going again, after they had grown rusty and tired during recent weeks. I had become so used to talking everything over with you that the sudden and prolonged interruption meant a profound change and a great deprivation. Now we are at least in touch again. ... Roeder & Co. have smashed so much china already that we must not let them destroy our most important personal relationships too.

.... And now I am taking up with great pleasure your "fireside chat" (appropriately enough the electricity has failed again, and I am using candles). So I imagine the two of us sitting together as we used to in the old days after supper (and after our regular evening's work[14]) in my room upstairs, smoking, occasionally playing chords on the clavichord, and discussing the day's events. I should have no end of questions to ask you, about your training, about your journey to Karolus[15] ... And then at last I should have to start telling you that, in spite of everything that I have so far written, things here are revolting, that my grim experiences often pursue me into the night and that I can shake them off only by reciting one hymn after another, and that I am apt to wake up with a sigh rather than with a hymn of praise to God. It is possible to get used to physical hardships, and to live for months out of the body, so to speak—almost too much so—but one does not get used to the psychological strain; on the contrary, I have the feeling that everything that I see and hear is putting years on me, and that I am often finding the world nauseating and burdensome. You are probably surprised now at my

[14] Listening to foreign broadcasts.
[15] Karl Barth.

talking like this after all my letters; you wrote very kindly that I was making "something of an effort" to reassure you about my situation. I often wonder who I really am—the man who goes on squirming under these ghastly experiences in wretchedness that cries to heaven, or the man who scourges himself and pretends to others (and even to himself) that he is placid, cheerful, composed, and in control of himself, and allows people to admire him for it (i.e. for playing the part— or is it not playing a part?). What does one's attitude mean, anyway? In short, I know less than ever about myself, and I am no longer attaching any importance to it. I have had more than enough psychology, and I am less and less inclined to analyse the state of my soul. That is why I value Stifter and Gotthelf so much. There is something more at stake than self-knowledge.

Then I should discuss with you whether you think that this trial, which has associated me with the Security Branch Resistance Movement (I hardly think that has remained a secret) may prevent me from taking up my ministry again later on. At present you are the only person with whom I can discuss this question, and perhaps we shall be able to talk it over together if you are allowed to see me. Please think it over, and give me your candid opinion.

. . . I sometimes feel as if my life were more or less over, and as if all I had to do now were to finish my *Ethics*. But, you know, when I feel like this, there comes over me a longing (unlike any other that I experience) not to vanish without a trace—an Old Testament rather than a New Testament wish, I suppose. . . .

. . . If only we could meet in freedom before you leave. But if they really intend to keep me here over Christmas, I shall keep it in my own way as a Christmas at the front, so you can have an easy mind about it. Great battles are easier to fight and less wearing than the daily guerrilla war. And I do hope you will somehow or other manage to wangle a few days' leave in February; I shall certainly be out of here by then, for, to judge by the nonsense that they are bringing against me, they are bound to let me out when the time is up.

I am again working at my essay on "What is 'speaking the truth?' " I am trying to draw a sharp contrast between trust, loyalty, and secrecy on the one hand, and the "cynical" conception of truth, for which all these obligations do not exist, on the other. "Falsehood" is the destruction of, and hostility to, reality as it is in God; anyone who tells the truth cynically is lying. By the way, it is remarkable how little I miss going to church. I wonder why.

Your biblical comparison with "eating the letter" is very good. If you should get to Rome, do visit Sch.[16] in the *Propaganda Fide.*—Have you found the tone among the troops very bad, or do they show you some respect? Here in the sick-bay the men are certainly very direct, but not smutty. Some of the younger prisoners seem to have suffered so much from the long solitary confinement and the long dark evenings that they have quite gone to pieces. That is another idiotic thing, locking these people in for months on end with nothing to do; it is absolutely demoralizing in every possible way. . . .

18 December 1943

You too must at least have a letter for Christmas. I am no longer expecting to be released. As far as I could see, I should have been released on 17 December, but the . . . wanted to take the safe course, and now I shall probably be kept here for weeks if not months.

---

[16] Mgr. Dr. Johann Schönhöffer of the *Propaganda Fide* in the Vatican.

The past weeks have been more of a strain than anything before that. There is no changing it, only it is
more difficult to adapt oneself to something that one
thinks could have been prevented than to something
inevitable. But when facts have taken shape, one just
has to fit in with them. What I am thinking of particularly today is that you will soon be facing facts that will
be very hard for you, probably even harder than for
me. I now think that we ought first of all to do everything we can to change those facts while there is still
time; and then, if we have tried everything, even though
it has been in vain, they will be much easier to bear.
Of course, not everything that happens is simply "God's
will," and yet in the last resort nothing happens "without your Father's will" (Matt. 10.29), i.e. through
every event, however untoward, there is access to God.
When a man enters on a supremely happy marriage
and has thanked God for it, it is a terrible blow to discover that the same God who established the marriage
now demands of us a period of such great deprivation.
In my experience nothing tortures us more than longing. Some people have been so violently shaken in
their lives from their earliest days that they cannot now,
so to speak, allow themselves any great longing or put
up with a long period of tension, and they find compen-
sation in short-lived pleasures that offer readier satisfaction. That is the fate of the proletarian classes, and
it is the ruin of all intellectual fertility. It is not true to
say that it is good for a man to have suffered heavy
blows early and often in life; in most cases it breaks
him. True, it hardens people for times like ours, but it
also greatly helps to deaden them. When *we* are forci-
bly separated for any considerable time from those
whom we love, we simply *cannot*, as most can, get
some cheap substitute through other people—I don't
mean because of moral considerations, but just because

we are what we are. Substitutes repel us; we simply
have to wait and wait; we have to suffer unspeakably
from the separation, and feel the longing till it almost
makes us ill. That is the only way, although it is a very
painful one, in which we can preserve unimpaired our
relationship with our loved ones. A few times in my
life I have come to know what homesickness means.
There is nothing more painful, and during these months
in prison I have sometimes been terribly homesick. And
as I expect you will have to go through the same kind
of thing in the coming months, I wanted to write and
tell you what I have learnt about it, in case it may be
of some help to you. The first result of such longing is
always a wish to neglect the ordinary daily routine in
some way or other, and that means that our lives become disordered. I used to be tempted sometimes to
stay in bed after six in the morning (it would have
been perfectly possible), and to sleep on. Up to now
I have always been able to force myself not to do this;
I realized that it would have been the first stage of
capitulation, and that worse would probably have followed. An outward and purely physical régime (exer-
cises and a cold wash down in the morning) itself
provides some support for one's inner discipline. Further, there is nothing worse in such times than to try
to find a substitute for the irreplaceable. It just does not
work, and it leads to still greater indiscipline, for the
strength to overcome tension (such strength can come
only from looking the longing straight in the face) is
impaired, and endurance becomes even more unbear-
able. . . .

Another point: I don't think it is good to talk to
strangers about our condition; that always stirs up one's
troubles—although we ought to be ready, when occasion arises, to listen to those of other people. Above
all, we must never give way to self-pity. And on the

Christian aspect of the matter, there are some lines that
say

> *. . . dass nicht vergessen werde,*
> *was man so gern vergisst,*
> *dass diese arme Erde*
> *nicht unsre Heimat ist.*[17]

That is indeed something essential, but it must come
last of all. I believe that we ought so to love and trust
God in our *lives*, and in all the good things that he
sends us, that when the time comes (but not before!)
we may go to him with love, trust, and joy. But, to
put it plainly, for a man in his wife's arms to be
hankering after the other world is, in mild terms, a
piece of bad taste, and not God's will. We ought to
find and love God in what he actually gives us; if it
pleases him to allow us to enjoy some overwhelming
earthly happiness, we must not try to be more pious
than God himself and allow our happiness to be cor-
rupted by presumption and arrogance, and by unbridled
religious fantasy which is never satisfied with what God
gives. God will see to it that the man who finds him in
his earthly happiness and thanks him for it does not
lack reminder that earthly things are transient, that it
is good for him to attune his heart to what is eternal,
and that sooner or later there will be times when he
can say in all sincerity, "I wish I were home." But everything has its time, and the main thing is that we
keep step with God, and do not keep pressing on a
few steps ahead—nor keep dawdling a step behind. It
is presumptuous to want to have everything at once—
matrimonial bliss, the cross, and the heavenly Jeru-
salem, where they neither marry nor are given in mar-

[17] "That we may remember what we so like to forget—that
this poor earth is not our home." (From the hymn *Das Jahr
geht still zu Ende* by Eleonore Fürstin Reuss.)

riage. "For everything there is a season" (Eccles. 3.1);
everything has its time: "a time to weep, and a time to
laugh; . . . a time to embrace, and a time to refrain
from embracing; . . . a time to rend, and a time to
sew; . . . and God seeks what has been driven away."
These last words probably mean that nothing that is
past is lost, that God gathers up again with us our
past, which belongs to us. So when we are seized by a
longing for the past—and this may happen when we
least expect it—we may be sure that it is only one of
the many "hours" that God is always holding ready for
us. So we ought not to seek the past again by our own
efforts, but only with God. Well, enough of this; I can
see that I have taken on too much, for really in these
matters I can tell you nothing that you don't know
already.

Advent IV

. . . For this last week or so these lines have kept on
running through my head:

> *Lasset fahr'n, o liebe Brüder,*
> *was euch quält, was euch fehlt;*
> *ich bring alles wieder.*[18]

What does this "I will restore" mean? It means that
nothing is lost, that everything is taken up in Christ,
although it is transformed, made transparent, clear,
and free from all selfish desire. Christ restores all this
as God originally intended it to be, without the distor-
tion resulting from our sins. The doctrine derived from
Eph. 1.10—that of the restoration of all things,
ἀνακεφαλαίωσις, *recapitulatio* (Irenaeus)—is a magnifi-

---

[18] "Let go, dear brothers, every pain and every want; I will
restore everything." (From *Frohlich soll mein Herze springen*,
by Paul Gerhardt.)

cent conception, full of comfort. This is how the promise "God seeks what has been driven away" is fulfilled.
And no one has expressed this so simply and artlessly
as Paul Gerhardt in the words that he puts into the
mouth of the Christ-child: *Ich bring alles wieder*. Perhaps this line will help you a little in the coming weeks.
Besides that, I have lately learnt for the first time to
appreciate the hymn *Ich steh an deiner Krippe hier*
. . .[19] Up to now I had not made much of it; I suppose
one has to be alone for a long time, and meditate on it,
to be able to take it in properly. Every word is remarkably full of meaning and beauty. There is just a slight
flavour of the monastery and mysticism, but no more
than is justified. After all, it is right to speak of "I"
and "Christ" as well as of "we," and what that means
can hardly be expressed better than it is in this hymn.
There are also a few passages in a similar vein in the
Imitation of Christ, which I am reading now and then
in the Latin (it reads much better in Latin than in German); and I sometimes think of

from the Augustinian *O bone Jesu* by Schütz. Does not
this passage, in its ecstatic longing combined with pure
devotion, suggest the "restoration" of all earthly desire? "Restoration," of course must not be confused
with "sublimation"; "sublimation" is σάρξ, "flesh" (and
pietistic?), and "restoration" is spirit, not in the sense
of "spiritualization" (which is also σάρξ), but of καινὴ
κτίσις through the πνεῦμα ἅγιον, a new creation through
the Holy Spirit. I think this point is also very important when we have to talk to people who ask us about
their relation to their dead. "I will restore everything"

[19] "Before thy cradle here I stand. . . ." (Paul Gerhardt.)

—that is, we cannot and should not take it back ourselves, but allow Christ to give it back to us. (By the
way, I should like the choir to sing at my funeral *Eins
bitte ich vom Herren,*[20] *Eile, mich, Gott, zu erretten,*[21]
and *O bone Jesu.*[22])

At midday on Christmas Eve a dear old man is coming here at his own suggestion to play some Christmas
carols on a cornet. But some people with good judgment think it only makes the prisoners thoroughly unhappy, and so makes the day even harder for them;
one said that the effect is "demoralizing," and I can
well imagine it. In former years the prisoners are said
to have whistled and kicked up a row, no doubt to
stop themselves from becoming sentimental. I think,
too, that in view of all the misery that prevails here,
anything like a pretty-pretty, sentimental reminder of
Christmas is out of place. A good personal message, a
sermon, would be better; without something of the kind,
music by itself may be positively dangerous. Please
don't think that I am in any way frightened of that for
myself; I am not, but I am sorry for all those helpless
young soldiers in their cells. One will probably never
quite get rid of the accumulated weight of all the oppressive experiences that come day after day, and I
suppose it is right that that should be so. I am thinking
a great deal about a radical reform of the penal system,
and I hope my ideas may be turned to account some
day.

If this letter reaches you in time, please try to get
me something good to read over Christmas. I asked for
a few books some time ago, but they may not have
been available. Something exciting would do quite well.
And if you can get without difficulty Barth's *Doctrine*

20 "One thing have I asked of the Lord" (Ps. 27.4).
21 "O Lord, make haste to help me" (Ps. 40.13).
22 The settings by Heinrich Schütz.

of Predestination (in sheets), or his *Doctrine of God*,[23] please let me have them too. . . .

The propagandist with whom I walk every day is really getting more and more difficult to put up with. Whereas most people here do try to keep control of themselves, even in the most difficult cases, he has completely gone to pieces, and cuts a really sorry figure. I try to be as nice as I can to him, and talk to him as if he were a child. Sometimes he is almost comical. What is pleasanter is to hear that when I am in the sick-bay in the afternoon the word goes round the kitchen or the garden, and the prisoners come up on some pretext or other because, they say, it is so nice to have a chat with me. Of course, that is not really allowed, but I was pleased to hear about it, and I am sure you will be too. But mind you don't let it get around.—This is probably the last chance we shall have for some time of writing each other uncensored letters. . . .

No more for now. Read Proverbs 18.24, and don't forget it.

22 December 1943

They seem to have made up their minds that I am not to be with you for Christmas, though no one ventures to tell me so. I wonder why; do they think I am so easily upset? . . . The English have a very suitable word for this sort of thing—"tantalizing" . . . I do want to convey to you somehow tomorrow that I believe my attitude towards my case ought unquestionably to be one of faith, and I feel that it has become too much a matter of calculation and foresight. I am not so much concerned about the rather artless question whether I shall be home for Christmas or not; I think I could willingly renounce that, if I could do so

[23] *Church Dogmatics*, Vol. II, Parts 1 and 2, sent from Switzerland without title and cover, as they were banned in Germany.

"in faith," knowing that it was inevitable. I can (I hope) bear all things "in faith," even my condemnation, and even the other consequences that I fear (Ps. 18.29); but to be anxiously looking ahead wears one down. Don't worry about me if something worse happens.[24] Others of the brethren have already been through that. But faithless vacillation, endless deliberation without action, refusal to take any risks—that is a real danger. I must be able to know for certain that I am in God's hands, not in men's. Then everything becomes easy, even the severest privation. It is not now a matter (I think I can say this truthfully) of my being "understandably impatient," as people are probably saying, but of my facing everything in faith. . . .

Now I want to assure you that I have not for a moment regretted coming back in 1939[25]—nor any of the consequences, either. I knew quite well what I was doing, and I acted with a clear conscience. I have no wish to cross out of my life anything that has happened since, either to me personally . . . Sigurdshof, East Prussia, et. al., my illness and all the help you gave me then, and the time in Berlin), or as regards events in general. And I regard my being kept here (do you remember that I prophesied to you last March about what the year would bring?) as being involved in the part that I had resolved to play in Germany's fate. It is with no reproach that I look back on the past and accept the present, but I do not want the machinations of men to make me waver. All we can do is to live in assurance and faith—you out there with the soldiers, and I in my cell.—I have just come across this in the *Imitation of Christ: Custodi diligenter cellam tuam, et custodiet te* ("Take good care of your cell, and it will take care of you").—May God keep us in faith.

---

[24] Possible removal to a concentration camp.
[25] See p. xix.

Christmas Eve, 1943

It is half past nine in the evening; I have been spending a few lovely peaceful hours, and thinking very thankfully about your being able to spend the day together. . . .

One of my greatest joys this Christmas is that we have again been able to exchange the *Losungen*[26] for the coming year. I had already thought of it and hoped for it, though I hardly thought it would be possible. And now this book, which has meant so much to me in the past months, will be with us throughout next year too, and when we read it in the morning we shall think especially of each other. Many, many thanks. . . .

I should like to say something to help you in the time of separation that lies ahead. There is no need to say how hard any such separation is for us; but as I have now been separated for nine months from all the people that I am devoted to, I should like to pass on to you something of what I have learnt. . . .

First: nothing can make up for the absence of someone whom we love, and it would be wrong to try to find a substitute; we must simply hold out and see it through. That sounds very hard at first, but at the same time it is a great consolation, for the gap, as long as it remains unfilled, preserves the bonds between us. It is nonsense to say that God fills the gap; he does not fill it, but on the contrary, he keeps it empty and so helps us to keep alive our former communion with each other, even at the cost of pain.

Secondly: the dearer and richer our memories, the more difficult the separation. But gratitude changes the pangs of memory into a tranquil joy. The beauties of the past are borne, not as a thorn in the flesh, but as a precious gift in themselves. We must take care not to

[26] *Die täglichen Losungen und Lehrtexte der Brüdergemeinde*, published yearly since 1731.

wallow in our memories or hand ourselves over to them, just as we do not gaze all the time at a valuable present, but only at special times, and apart from these keep it simply as a hidden treasure that is ours for certain. In this way the past gives us lasting joy and strength.

Thirdly: times of separation are not a total loss or unprofitable for our companionship, or at any rate they need not be so. In spite of all the difficulties that they bring, they can be the means of strengthening fellowship quite remarkably.

Fourthly: I have learnt here especially that the *facts* can always be mastered, and that difficulties are magnified out of all proportion simply by fear and anxiety. From the moment we wake until we fall asleep we must commend other people wholly and unreservedly to God and leave them in his hands, and transform our anxiety for them into prayers on their behalf:

> *Mit Sorgen und mit Grämen. . . .*
> *lässt Gott sich gar nichts nehmen*[27] *. . .*

Christmas Day

. . . Once more all my beautiful presents are arranged on the edge of my tipped-up bed, and in front of me are the pictures that I enjoy so much. I am still relishing, almost uninterruptedly, the memory of your visit. . . . It really was a *necessitas*. The mind's hunger for discussion is much more tormenting than the body's hunger for food. . . . A few pregnant remarks are enough to touch on a wide range of questions and clear them up. This ability to keep on the same wavelength, to play to each other, took years to cultivate, not always without friction, and we must never lose it. It is an incredible gain, and extraordinarily helpful. What a

[27] "With cares and grief . . . God *will not* be received" (from *Befiehl du deine Wege*, by Paul Gerhardt).

great deal we touched on in that hour and a half, and how much we learnt from each other! Thank you very much for arranging the meeting successfully. . . .

. . . The people here did their best to give me a happy Christmas, but I was glad to be alone again; I was surprised at that, and I sometimes wonder how I shall adapt myself to company again after this. You know how I used occasionally to retire to my own room after some great celebration. I am afraid I must have grown even worse, for in spite of all my privations I have come to love solitude. I very much like to talk with two or three people, but I detest anything like a large assembly, and above all any chatter or gossip. . . .

23 January 1944

Since you left for the front[28] on 9 January my thoughts about you have taken a new shape. . . . That Sunday was a wrench for me as well as for you, though in a different way. It is a strange feeling to see a man whose life has in one way or another been so intimately bound up with one's own for years going out to meet an unknown future about which one can do virtually nothing. I think this realization of one's own helplessness has . . . two sides—it brings both anxiety and relief. As long as we ourselves are trying to help shape someone else's destiny, we are never quite free of the question whether what we are doing is really for the other person's benefit—at least in any matter of great importance. But when all possibility of co-operating in anything is suddenly cut off, then behind any anxiety about him there is the consciousness that his life has now been placed wholly in better and stronger hands. For you, and for us, the greatest task during the coming weeks, and perhaps months, may be to entrust each other to those hands. Whatever weaknesses, miscalcula-

[28] In Italy.

tions, and guilt there is in what precedes the facts, God
is in the facts themselves. If we survive during these
coming weeks or months, we shall be able to see quite
clearly that all has turned out for the best. The idea
that we could have avoided many of life's difficulties if
we had taken things more cautiously is too foolish to
be entertained for a moment. As I look back on your
past I am so convinced that what has happened hitherto
has been right, that I feel that what is happening now
is right too. To renounce a full life and its real joys in
order to avoid pain is neither Christian nor human. . . .

The news of the Nettuno landing has just come. I
wonder whether you are anywhere thereabouts. When
things like this happen, I see that composure is not
part of my nature, but that I have to acquire it at the
cost of repeated effort. In fact, natural composure is
probably in most cases nothing but a euphemism for
indifference and indolence, and to that extent it is not
very estimable. I read in Lessing recently: "I am too
proud to consider myself unlucky. Just clench your
teeth and let your skiff sail where the wind and waves
take it. Enough that I do not intend to upset it myself." Is this pride and teeth-clenching to be forbidden
to the Christian, and replaced, shall we say, by a soft
composure that gives way prematurely? Is there not
also a kind of composure which proudly clenches its
teeth, but is quite different from a dull, stolid, rigid,
lifeless, mechanical submitting-to-something-I-can't-
help? I think we honour God more if we gratefully accept the life that he gives us with all its blessings, loving
it and drinking it to the full, and also grieving deeply
and sincerely when we have impaired or wasted any of
the good things of life (some people denounce such an
attitude, and think it is bourgeois, weak, and sensitive),
than if we are insensitive to life's blessings and may
therefore also be insensitive to pain. Job's words, "The
Lord gave . . ." (1.21) include rather than exclude

this, as can be seen clearly enough from his teeth-clenching speeches which were vindicated by God (42.7ff.) in face of the false, premature, pious submission of his friends. . . .

. . . I very much agree with what you say in this connection about friendship, which, in contrast to marriage and kinship, has no generally recognized rights, and therefore depends entirely on its own inherent quality. It is by no means easy to classify friendship sociologically. Perhaps it is to be regarded as a sub-heading of culture and education, brotherhood being a sub-heading of church, and comradeship a sub-heading of work and politics. Marriage, work, state, and church all have their definite, divine mandate; but what about culture and education? I don't think they can just be classified under work, however tempting that might be in many ways. They belong, not to the sphere of obedience, but to the broad area of freedom, which surrounds all three spheres of the divine mandates. The man who is ignorant of this area of freedom may be a good father, citizen, and worker, indeed even a Christian; but I doubt whether he is a complete man and therefore a Christian in the widest sense of the term. Our "Protestant" (not Lutheran) Prussian world has been so dominated by the four mandates that the area of freedom has receded into the background. I wonder whether it is possible (it almost seems so today) to regain the idea of the *Church* as providing an understanding of the area of freedom (art, education, friendship, play), so that Kirkegaard's "aesthetic existence" would not be banished from the Church's sphere, but would be reestablished within it? I really think that is so, and it would mean that we should recover a link with the Middle Ages. Who is there, for instance, in our times, who can devote himself with an easy mind to music, friendship, games, or happiness? Surely not the

The school (left) at Schönberg where Bonhoeffer was housed for a few days before execution and where he conducted a service on Easter Day 1945

The "courtroom"—hastily improvised from the laundry at Flossenbürg extermination camp

Flossenbürg camp: the steps down from the living quarters to the execution area

Bonhoeffer with his parents

Eberhard Bethge and Bonhoeffer

Tegel Prison where Bonhoeffer was kept from April 1943 until October 1944. Bonhoeffer's cell is the fifth window from the right in the top row.

The ruins of the Gestapo Headquarters in Prinz-Albrecht-Strasse, Berlin. Bonhoeffer was transferred here from Tegel Prison and was kept for a time in bunker 3—left of the picture.

"ethical" man, but only the Christian. Just because friendship belongs to this sphere of freedom ("of the Christian man?!"), it must be confidently defended against all the disapproving frowns of "ethical" existences, though without claiming for it the *necessitas* of a divine decree, but only the *necessitas* of freedom. I believe that within the sphere of this freedom friendship is by far the rarest and most priceless treasure, for where else does it survive in this world of ours, dominated as it is by the *three other* mandates? It cannot be compared with the treasures of the mandates, for in relation to them it is *sui generis*; it belongs to them as the cornflower belongs to the cornfield.

As to what you said about "Christ's anxiety": it comes out only in the *prayer* (as it does in the Psalms).[29] (I have never been clear why the evangelists report this prayer, which no one can have heard. The suggestion that Jesus revealed it to the disciples during the forty days is an evasion of the difficulty. Have you any comment?)

Your reference to Socrates' remarks about culture and death may be very valuable; I must think about it. The only thing I am really clear about in the whole problem is that a "culture" that breaks down in the face of danger is no culture. Culture must be able to face danger and death—*impavidum feriunt ruinae*: "the ruins will strike a fearless man" (Horace)—even if it cannot "conquer" them; what does "conquer" mean? By finding forgiveness in judgment, and joy in terror? But we must discuss this further. . . .

What will happen to Rome? The thought that it might be destroyed is a nightmare. What a good thing we saw it in peacetime!

I am getting on all right, working and waiting. Noth-

[29] Ps. 22.1.

ing has happened to shake my optimism, and I hope it is the same with you. Goodbye; may we soon meet again happily!

If you see the Laocoon again, just notice whether you do not think that the father's head may have been the model for later representations of Christ. Last time I saw this classical man of sorrows it impressed me deeply and kept me thinking for a long time. . . .

. . . I have had to take a new line with the companion of my daily walks. Although he has done his best to ingratiate himself with me, he let fall a remark about the Jewish problem lately that has made me more offhanded and cool to him than I have ever been to anyone before; and I have also seen to it that he has been deprived of certain little comforts. Now he feels obliged to go round whimpering for a time, but it leaves me—I am surprised myself, but interested too— absolutely cold. He really is a pitiful figure, but certainly not "poor Lazarus."

29 and 30 January 1944

. . . and as I find it hard not to write to you, I am using this quiet Saturday afternoon, so very different from the din that we have had the last two nights, to talk some things over with you. I wonder how the first few days of direct contact with war, and possibly your first personal impressions of the Anglo-Saxon opponents, whom we have so far met only in times of peace, have affected you . . .

When I think of you every morning and evening, I have to try very hard not to let all my thoughts dwell on the many cares and anxieties that beset you, instead of praying for you properly. In that connection I must talk to you some time about prayer in time of trouble; it is a difficult matter, and yet our misgivings about it may not be good. Psalm 50 says quite clearly, "Call upon me in the day of trouble; I will deliver you, and you shall glorify me." The whole history of the children of Israel consists of such cries for help. And I must say that the last two nights have made me face this problem again in a quite elementary way. While the bombs are falling like that all round the building, I cannot help thinking of God, his judgment, his hand stretched out and his anger not turned away (Isa. 5.25 and 9.11–10.4), and of my own unpreparedness. I feel how men can make vows, and then I think of you all and say, "better me than one of them"—and that makes me realize how attached I am to you all. I won't say anything more about it—it will have to be by word of mouth; but when all is said and done, it is true that it needs trouble to shake us up and drive us to prayer, though I feel every time that it is something to be ashamed of, as indeed it is. That may be because I have not up to now felt able to put in a Christian word to the others at such a moment. As we were again lying on the floor last night, and some one exclaimed "O God, O God" (he is normally a very flippant fellow), I could not bring myself to offer him any Christian encouragement or comfort; all I did was to look at my watch and say, "It won't last more than ten minutes now." There was nothing premeditated about it; it came quite automatically, and perhaps I felt that it was wrong to force religion down his throat just then. (Incidentally, Jesus did not try to convert the two thieves on the cross; one of them turned to him.)

I am sorry to say that I suffered a severe loss the night before last. The man who was, to my mind, by far the most intelligent and attractive in the place was killed in the city by a direct hit. I should certainly have put him in touch with you later, and we already had plans for the future. We often had interesting talks, and the other day he brought me *Daumier und die Justiz*, which I still have. He was a really educated man of working-class origin, a philosopher, and father of three children. I was very much distressed by his death.

In the last few days I have again been busy on the little work that I mentioned to you before, about the meeting of two old friends after they had been separated for a long time during the war. I hope to be able to send it to you soon. You needn't worry—it will *not* be a *roman à clef*.[30]

. . . In earlier times even one of the problems that we are now having to deal with would have been enough to take up all our time. Now we have to reduce to a common denominator war, marriage, church, profession, housing, the possible death of those nearest and dearest to us, and, added to that, my present situation. No doubt most people would regard these simply as separate problems, but for the Christian and the "cultured" man that is impossible; he cannot split up his life or dismember it, and the common denominator must be sought both in thought and in a personal and integrated attitude to life. The man who allows himself to be torn into fragments by events and by questions has not passed the test for the present and the future. In the story of young Witiko we read that he set out into the world "*um das Ganze zu tun*" (to do the whole thing); here we have the ἄνθρωπος τέλειος (τέλειος originally meant "whole" in the sense of "complete" or "perfect"); "You, therefore, must be perfect (τέλειος), as your heavenly Father is perfect" (Matt. 5.48)—in contrast to the ἀνὴρ δίψυχος ("a double-minded man") of James 1.8. Witiko "does the whole thing" by trying to adapt himself to the realities of life, by always listening to the advice of experienced people—i.e. by showing that he is one of those who are "whole." We can never achieve this "wholeness" simply by ourselves, but only together with others. . . .

I have just started to read Harnack's *Geschichte der*

---

[30] A type of novel which depicts an actual situation, but in which all the characters are disguised.

Preussischen Akademie; it is very good. I am sure he put his heart and soul into it, and he said more than once that he considered it his best book.—How are you? Do let me know. I am still surprisingly well. I suppose it makes some difference to know that I must not be ill here in any circumstances. I always find enough strength and concentration for reading, but not always for writing and constructive work, except now and again. How I shall get used to living in company again I don't yet know. . . .

1 February 1944

Carpe diem—which in this case means that I take every chance of sending you a greeting. First, because I could write for weeks on end without finishing all that I have to tell you, and secondly, because one never knows how much longer things are likely to last. . . .

You may know that the last few nights have been bad, especially the night of 30 January. Those who had been bombed out came to me the next morning for a bit of comfort. But I am afraid I am bad at comforting; I can listen all right, but I can hardly ever find anything to say. But perhaps the way one asks about some things and not about others helps to suggest what really matters; and it seems to me more important actually to share someone's distress than to use smooth words about it. I have no sympathy with some wrong-headed attempts to explain away distress, because instead of being a comfort, they are the exact opposite. So I do not try to explain it, and I think that is the right way to begin, although it is only a beginning, and I very seldom get beyond it. I sometimes think that real comfort must break in just as unexpectedly as the distress. But I admit that that may be a subterfuge.

Something that repeatedly puzzles me as well as other people is how quickly we forget about our impressions of a night's bombing. Even a few minutes after the all clear, almost everything that we had just been thinking about seems to vanish into thin air. With Luther a flash of lightning was enough to change the course of his life for years to come. Where is this "memory" today? Is not the loss of this "moral memory" (a horrid expression) responsible for the ruin of all obligations, of love, marriage, friendship, and loyalty? Nothing sticks fast, nothing holds firm; everything is here today and gone tomorrow. But the good things of life—truth, justice, and beauty—all great accomplishments need time, constancy, and "memory," or they degenerate. The man who feels neither responsibility towards the past nor desire to shape the future is one who "forgets," and I do not know how one can really get at such a person and bring him to his senses. Every word, even if it impresses him for the moment, goes in at one ear and out at the other. What is to be done about him? It is a great problem of Christian ministry. You put it very well recently when you said that people feel so quickly and so "shamelessly at home"; I am going to crib that expression from you, and make good use of it. . . .

By the way, do you notice that uneducated people find it very difficult to decide things *objectively*, and that they allow some more or less fortuitous minor circumstance to turn the scales? It seems to me quite remarkable. I suppose one first has to take pains to *learn* to distinguish between thinking personally and thinking objectively; and, in fact, many people never learn to do so. . . .

2 February 1944

Is it true that you are north of Rome? I hope you will have a chance to see the place again; it must be tantalizing to be stationed outside the gates, and not be allowed to go in. It is not much consolation that you have already seen it once. . . .

How much longer I shall have to go on enjoying myself in my present place of residence is still just as uncertain as it was eight weeks ago. I am using every day to do as much reading and work as possible, for what will happen afterwards is anybody's guess. Unfortunately the one thing I cannot do is to get hold of the right books, and that upsets all my plans. I really wanted to become thoroughly familiar with the nineteenth century in Germany. I am now feeling particularly the need of a good working knowledge of Dilthey, but his books are obviously not available. It is a matter of great regret to me that I am so ignorant of the natural sciences, but it is a gap that cannot be filled now.

My present companion, whom I have mentioned several times in my letters, gets more and more pitiable. He has two colleagues here, one of whom spends the whole day moaning, and the other literally messes his trousers whenever the alarm goes, and last night even when the alert was sounded! When he told me about it yesterday—still moaning—I laughed outright and told him off, whereupon he would have me know that one must not laugh at anyone in distress or condemn him. I felt that that was really going too far, and I told him in no uncertain terms what I thought of people who can be very hard on others and talk big about a dangerous life and so on, and then collapse under the slightest test of endurance. I told him that it was a downright disgrace, that I had no sympathy at all with anyone like that, that I would throw any such specimens out of the party for making it look ridiculous, and so on. He was very surprised, and I dare say he thinks me a very doubtful Christian. Anyhow, these gentlemen's behaviour is already becoming a byword here, and the result cannot be exactly pleasant for them. I find all this uncommonly instructive, though it is one of the most nauseating things that I have seen here so

far. I don't really think I find it easy to despise anyone
in trouble, and I said so quite unmistakably, which
may have made his hair stand on end; but I can only
regard that as contemptible. There are 17–18-year-olds
here in much more dangerous places during the raids
who behave splendidly, while these . . . (I almost used
an army term that would have surprised you) go round
whimpering. It really makes one sick. Well, everyone
makes a fool of himself as best he can.

I hope you won't think I've joined the ranks of the
toughs; there is little enough occasion for that here, in
any case. But there is a kind of weakness that Christianity does not hold with, but which people insist on
claiming as Christian, and then sling mud at it. So we
must take care that the contours do not get blurred.

Yesterday S[usanne] brought me the big volume on
Magdeburg Cathedral. I am quite thrilled by the sculptures, especially some of the wise virgins. The bliss on
these very earthly, almost peasant-like faces is really
delightful and moving. Of course, you will know them
well.

4 February 1944

Today on my birthday morning, nothing is more natural for me than to write to you, remembering that for
eight years in succession we celebrated the day together.
Work is being laid aside for a few hours—it may take
no harm from that—and I am expecting a visit from
M[aria] or my parents, although it is not yet quite certain whether it will come off. Eight years ago we were
sitting at the fireside together. You had given me as a
present the D major violin concerto, and we listened
to it together; then I had to tell you a little about Harnack and past times; for some reason or other you enjoyed that very much, and afterwards we decided
definitely to go to Sweden. A year later you gave me

the September Bible[81] with a lovely inscription and
your name at the top. There followed Schlönwitz and
Sigurdshof,[82] and we had the company of a good many
people who are no longer among us.[83] The singing at
the door, the prayer at the service that you undertook
that day, the Claudius hymn,[84] for which I am in-
debted to G.[85]—all those things are delightful recollec-
tions that are proof against the horrible atmosphere of
this place. I hope confidently that we shall be together
again for your next birthday, and perhaps—who
knows?—even for Easter. Then we shall get back to
what is really our life's work; we shall have ample work
that we shall enjoy, and what we have experienced in
the meantime will not have been in vain. We shall
probably always be grateful to each other for having
been able to go through this present time as we are
now doing. I know you are thinking of me today, and
if your thoughts include not only the past, but also the
hope of a future lived with a common purpose, even
though in changed circumstances, then indeed I am
happy.

Now it will not be long before you have good news
from R[enate]. It cannot be easy to have to celebrate
such a uniquely happy day among strangers who cannot help one to enjoy the occasion to the full and make
it part of one's ordinary life, and to whom the climax
of any happy occasion is probably the consumption of
alcohol. I wish very much that you could meet someone who has more in common with you (as I told you,
the only one here who seemed promising in that direc-

---

[81] Martin Luther's first complete translation of the Bible.
[82] Both in Pomerania.
[83] Because they had been killed in action.
[84] *Ich danke Gott und freue mich*, by Matthias Claudius.
[85] Gerhard Vibrans, Eberhard Bethge's cousin, killed in
Russia.

tion was killed in a raid), but I think that we, who have become more exacting than most people with regard to friendship, have more difficulty in finding what we miss and are looking for. In this respect, too, it is not a simple matter to find a substitute.

—When I was in the middle of this letter, I was called downstairs, where the first thing with which M[aria] greeted me was the happy news: "R[enate] has a little boy, and his name is Dietrich!" Everything went well; it took an hour and a half, and Mother acted as midwife, with C[hristine]'s help! What a surprise, and what a delight! I am happier than I can tell you. And how happy you, of all people, will be. And everything went so quickly and smoothly. So now you have a son, and all your thoughts will turn towards the future, full of hope. What possibilities there may be in him! . . . And so now he is really to be called Dietrich; I don't know what to say to that; I hope I can promise you to be a good godfather and "great-"uncle(!), and I should be insincere if I did not say that I am immensely pleased and proud that you have named your first-born after me. The fact that his birthday comes one day before mine means, no doubt, that he will keep his independence *vis-à-vis* his namesake-uncle, and will always be a little ahead of him. I am particularly pleased that the two days are so close to each other, and when he hears later on where his uncle was when he was told his name, perhaps that may leave some impression on him too. Thank you both very much for deciding to do this, and I think the others will be pleased about it too.

5 February. Yesterday, when so many people were showing such kindly concern for me, I completely forgot my own birthday, as my delight over little Dietrich's birthday put it right out of my head. Even the heartening little nosegay of flowers that some of my fellow inmates here picked for me remained in my thoughts by

your little boy's bed. The day could not possibly have
brought me any greater joy. It was not till I was going
to sleep that I realized that you have pushed our family on by one generation—3 February has created great-
grandparents, grandparents, great-uncles and great-
aunts, and young uncles and aunts! That is a fine
achievement of yours; you have promoted me to the
third generation! . . .

R[enate] sent me for my birthday yesterday some
more lovely home-made "S'le.[36] M[aria] brought a wonderful parcel, and my parents gave me the "Herzlieb-
chenschränken"[37] that Goethe once gave to Minna
Herzlieb. Klaus gave me Dilthey's *Von deutscher
Dichtung und Musik*; I will tell you about it later. Shall
you ask Mother and C[hristine] to be godparents? I am
sorry I must stop, as I want to send the letter off. My
head and my heart are so overflowing with good and
happy thoughts that I simply cannot put them all on
paper. But you know how I think about you and try
to share your joy with you and keep in close touch with
you. . . . Now I hope I shall soon follow your example. Good-bye, keep well; God keep and bless you
both, and the little boy.

12 February 1944

I have been in bed for a few days with slight influenza,
but I am up again; that is a good thing, because in
about a week's time I shall need to have all my wits
about me. Till then I shall go on reading and writing
as much as I can; who knows when I shall have another chance . . . ?

Are you having a taste of spring yet? Here the winter is just beginning. In my imagination I live a good

---

[36] A South German S-shaped Christmas biscuit.
[37] A beautiful little rosewood cupboard, which came from
Minna Herzlieb, through the von Hases, to the Bonhoeffers.

deal in nature, in the glades near Friedrichsbrunn, or on the slopes from which one can look beyond Trese-burg to the Brocken. I lie on my back in the grass, watch the clouds sailing in the breeze across the blue sky, and listen to the rustling of the woods. It is re-markable how greatly these memories of childhood af-fect one's whole outlook; it would seem to me impossible and unnatural for us to have lived either up in the mountains or by the sea. It is the hills of central Germany, the Harz, the Thuringian forest, the Weser-berge, that to me represent nature, that belong to me and have fashioned me. Of course, there are also a conventional Harz and a hikers' Wesergebirge, just as there are a fashionable and a Nietzschian Engadine, a romantic Rhineland, a Berliners' Baltic, and the ideal-ized poverty and melancholy of a fisherman's cottage. So perhaps "my" central hills are "bourgeois" in the sense of what is natural, not too high, modest and self-sufficient(?), unphilosophical, satisfied with concrete realities, and above all "not-given-to-self-advertise-ment." It would be very tempting to pursue this soci-ological treatment of nature some day. By the way, in reading Stifter I can see the difference between simple-ness and simplicity. Stifter displays, not simpleness, but (as the "bourgeois" does) simplicity. "Simpleness" is, even in theology, more of an aesthetic idea (was Winckelmann right when he spoke of the "noble sim-pleness" of classical art? That certainly does not apply to the Laocoon; I think "still greatness" is very good), whereas "simplicity" is an ethical one. One can acquire "simplicity," but "simpleness" is innate. Education and culture may bring "simplicity"—indeed, it ought to be one of their essential aims—but simpleness is a gift. The two things seem to me to be related in much the same way as "purity" and "moderation." One can be "pure" only in relation to one's origin or goal, i.e. in relation to baptism or to forgiveness at the Lord's Sup-

per; like "simpleness" it involves the idea of totality.
If we have lost our purity—and we have all lost it—it
can be given back to us in faith; but in ourselves, as
living and developing persons, we can no longer be
"pure," but only "moderate," and that is a possible
and a necessary aim of education and culture.

How does the Italian landscape impress you? Is
there any Italian school of landscape painters, anything
comparable to Thoma, or even to Claude Lorrain,
Ruysdael, or Turner? Or is nature there so completely
absorbed into art that it cannot be looked at for its
own sake? All the good pictures that I can think of just
now are of city life; I cannot remember any that are
purely of landscape.

13 February 1944

I often notice here, both in myself and in others, the
difference between the need to be communicative, the
wish for conversation, and the desire for confession.
The need to be communicative may perhaps on occasion be quite attractive in women, but I find it most
repugnant in men. There is quite indiscriminate gossip,
in front of all comers, about one's own affairs, no matter whether they interest or concern other people or
not—simply, in fact, because one just has to gossip. It
is an almost physical urge, but if you manage to suppress it for a few hours, you are glad afterwards that
you did not let yourself go. It sometimes makes me
ashamed here to see how people lower themselves in
their need to gossip, how they talk incessantly about
their own affairs to others who are hardly worth wast-
ing their breath on and who hardly even listen; and the
strange thing is that these people do not even feel that
they have to speak the truth, but simply want to talk
about themselves, whether they tell the truth or not.
The wish for a good conversation, a meeting of minds,
is quite another matter; but there are very few people

here who can carry on a conversation that goes beyond their own personal concerns.

Again, the desire for confession is something quite different. I think it is infrequent here, because people are not primarily concerned here, either subjectively or objectively, about "sin." You may perhaps have noticed that in the prayers that I sent you the request for forgiveness of sins does not occupy the central place; I should consider it a complete mistake, both from a pastoral and from a practical point of view, to proceed on "methodist" lines here. We must talk about that some day.

14 February 1944

. . . It looks as if something will be decided about me in a week's time. I hope it will. If it turns out that they send me in Martin's[38] direction (though I don't think that is likely), please make your mind easy about it. I am really not at all worried as to what happens to me personally. So please don't you worry either.

21 February 1944

. . . About myself, I am sorry to have to tell you that I am not likely to be out of here before Easter.

. . . I wonder whether my excessive scrupulousness, about which you often used to shake your head in amusement (I am thinking of our travels), is not a negative side of bourgeois existence—simply part of our lack of faith, a part that remains hidden in times of security, but comes out in times of insecurity in the form of "dread" (I don't mean "cowardice," which is something different: "dread" can show itself in recklessness as well as in cowardice), dread of straightforward, simple actions, dread of having to make necessary decisions. I have often wondered here where we are to

---

[38] Martin Niemöller, who was interned in the concentration camp at Dachau.

draw the line between necessary resistance to "fate," and equally necessary submission. Don Quixote is the symbol of resistance carried to the point of absurdity, even lunacy; and similarly Michael Kohlhaas, insisting on his rights, puts himself in the wrong . . . in both cases resistance at last defeats its own object, and evaporates in theoretical fantasy. Sancho Panza is the type of complacent and artful accommodation to things as they are. I think we must rise to the great demands that are made on us personally, and yet at the same time fulfil the commonplace and necessary tasks of daily life. We must confront fate—to me the neuter gender of the word "fate" (*Schicksal*) is significant— as resolutely as we submit to it at the right time. One can speak of "guidance" only on the other side of that twofold process, with God meeting us no longer as "Thou," but also "disguised" in the "It"; so in the last resort my question is how we are to find the "Thou" in this "It" (i.e. fate), or, in other words, how does "fate" really become "guidance?" It is therefore impossible to define the boundary between resistance and submission on abstract principles; but both of them must exist, and both must be practised. Faith demands this elasticity of behaviour. Only so can we stand our ground in each situation as it arises, and turn it to gain.

23 February 1944

If you have the chance of going to Rome during Holy Week, I advise you to attend the afternoon service at St. Peter's on Maundy Thursday (from about 2 to 6). That is really the Good Friday service, as the Roman Catholic Church anticipates its feasts from noon on the previous day. As far as I remember (though I am not quite certain), there is also a big service on the Wednesday. On Maundy Thursday the twelve candles on the altar are put out as a symbol of the disciples' flight, till in the vast space there is only one candle left

burning in the middle—for Christ. After that comes
the cleansing of the altar. At about 7 a.m. on the Saturday there is the blessing of the font (as far as I can
remember, that is connected with the ordination of
young priests). Then at 12 noon the Easter Alleluia is
sung, the organ plays again, the bells peal, and the pictures are unveiled. This is the real celebration of Easter.
Somewhere in Rome I also saw a Greek Orthodox service, which at the time—more than twenty years ago—
impressed me very much. The service on Easter Eve in
the Lateran (it starts in the Baptistery) is also very
famous. If you happen to be on Monte Pincio towards
sunset and are near the Church of Trinità del Monte,
do see whether the nuns are singing just then; I heard
them once, and was very impressed; I believe it is even
mentioned in Baedeker.

I wonder how far you are directly involved in the
fighting where you are. I suppose it is mainly a question of air raids, as it is here. The intensification of the
war in the air in about the last ten days, and especially
the heavy attacks in daylight, make one wonder whether
the English are probing our air power as a prelude to
invasion and as a means of pinning down our land
forces inside Germany.

The longer we are uprooted from our professional
activities and our private lives, the more we feel how
fragmentary our lives are, compared with those of our
parents. The portraits of the great savants in Harnack's
Geschichte der Akademie make me acutely aware of
that, and almost sadden me a little. Where is there today an intellectual *magnum opus*? Where are the collecting, assimilating, and sorting of material necessary
for producing such a work? Where is there today the
combination of fine *abandon* and large-scale planning
that goes with such a life? I doubt whether anything of
the kind still exists, even among technicians and scien-
tists, the only people who are still free to work in their

own way. The end of the eighteenth century saw the end of the "polymath," and in the nineteenth century intensive education replaced extensive, so that towards the end of it the "specialist" evolved; and by now everyone is just a technician, even in the arts—in music the standard is high, in painting and poetry extremely moderate. This means that our cultural life remains a torso. The important thing today is that we should be able to discern from the fragment of our life how the whole was arranged and planned, and what material it consists of. For really, there are some fragments that are only worth throwing into the dustbin (even a decent "hell" is too good for them), and others whose importance lasts for centuries, because their completion can only be a matter for God, and so they are fragments that must be fragments—I am thinking, e.g., of the art of the fugue. If our life is but the remotest reflection of such a fragment, if we accumulate, at least for a short time, a wealth of themes and weld them into a harmony in which the great counterpoint is maintained from start to finish, so that at last, when it breaks off abruptly, we can sing no more than the chorale, *Vor deinen Thron tret' ich allhier*,[39] we will not bemoan the fragmentariness of our life, but rather rejoice in it. I can never get away from Jeremiah 45. Do you still remember that Saturday evening in Finkenwalde when I expounded it? Here, too, is a necessary fragment of life—"but I will give you your life as a prize of war."

. . . I am very glad you have found someone more congenial than the ordinary run of people, for a companion to talk to and do things with. But I should very much prefer to be in his place. I wonder whether we shall ever manage it, or whether we may perhaps keep Easter here as we used to. You see I am not giving up hope; don't you give it up, either.

[39] "I come before thy throne" by J. S. Bach.

1 March 1944

. . . What a day it will be when we can discuss all
that we have been through and learnt during a whole
year. For myself at any rate, that is one of the greatest
hopes for the near future. I suppose you, too, can
sometimes hardly imagine that such a day will ever
come. It is difficult to believe that there is any chance
of our overcoming all the obstacles in our way, but
"that which tarries is all the sweeter when it comes."
. . . I must say I am entering on this new month with
great hopes, and I think you are doing the same. I am
redoubling my efforts to make the best use of the last
part of my time here. Perhaps your experiences, too,
will be of great value to you all your life. The constant
danger to which nearly all of us are at present exposed
in one way or another provides a wonderful incentive
to use the present moment, "making the most of the
time."[40] I sometimes feel that I am living just as long
as I have something great to work for. . . .

9 March 1944

I have heard from you . . . again today, that you are
at least finding things tolerable, and although that is
not very much (for we want life to be more than just
"tolerable"), it is some comfort, as long as we look on
our present condition as only a kind of *status inter-
medius*. If only we knew how long this purgatory is
going to last! It seems likely now that I shall have to
wait till May. Isn't this dawdling shameful?

. . . Sepp[41] is home again; he has fought his way
through with all his old resilience and defiance.

I have not yet answered your remarks about Michelangelo, Burckhardt, and *hilaritas*. I found them

[40] Eph. 5.16.
[41] Dr. Josef Müller of Munich, who had been acquitted, and
whom Bonhoeffer wrongly supposed to have been released.

illuminating—at any rate, what you say about Burck-hardt's theses. But surely *hilaritas* means not only serenity, in the classical sense of the word (Raphael and Mozart); Walther v.d. Vogelweide, the Knight of Bamberg, Luther, Lessing, Rubens, Hugo Wolf, Karl Barth—to mention only a few—also have a kind of *hilaritas*, which I might describe as confidence in their own work, boldness and defiance of the world and of popular opinion, a steadfast certainty that in their own work they are showing the world something *good* (even if the world does not like it), and a high-spirited self-confidence. I admit that Michelangelo, Rambrandt, and, at a considerable remove, Kirkegaard and Nietzsche, are in quite a different category from those that I have mentioned. There is something less assertive, evident, and final in their works, less conviction, detachment, and humour. All the same, I think some of them are characterized by *hilaritas* in the sense that I have described, as a necessary attribute of greatness. Here is Burckhardt's limitation, probably a conscious one.

I have recently been studying the mature "worldliness" of the thirteenth century, conditioned, not by the Renaissance, but by the Middle Ages, and presumably by the struggle between the idea of the Emperor and the papacy. (Walther, the Nibelungen, Parsifal—what surprising tolerance of the Mohammedans in the figure of Parsifal's half-brother Feirefiz!—Naumburg and Magdeburg cathedrals.) This worldliness is not "emancipated," but "Christian," even if it is anti-clerical. Where did this "worldliness," so essentially different from that of the Renaissance, stop? A trace of it seems to survive in Lessing—in contrast to the Western Enlightenment—and in a different way in Goethe, then later in Stifter and Mörike (to say nothing of Claudius and Gotthelf), but nowhere in Schiller and the Idealists. It would be very useful to draw up a good genealogy here; and that raises the question of the value of classi-

cal antiquity. Is this still a real problem and a source
of power for us, or not? The modern treatment of it
under the heading "city-state man" is already out of
date, and the classicists' treatment of it from the aesthetic point of view has only a limited appeal today,
and is something of a museum piece. The fundamental
concepts of humanism—humanity, tolerance, gentle-
ness, and moderation—are already present in their
finest form in Wolfram von Eschenbach and in the
Knight of Bamberg, and they are more accessible to us
here than in classical antiquity itself. How far, then,
does "education" still depend on classical antiquity? Is
the Ranke-to-Delbrück interpretation of history as a
continuum consisting of "classical antiquity," "the Middle Ages," and "modern times" really valid, or is not
Spengler also right with his theory of cultural phases
as self-contained cycles, even though he gives too bio-
logical a twist to historical events? The idea of the historical *continuum* goes back to Hegel, who sees the
whole course of history as culminating in "modern
times"—i.e. in his own system of philosophy. That idea
is therefore *idealistic* (in spite of Ranke's assertion
that every moment of history is "immediate to God";
that assertion might have supplied a corrective of the
whole conception of the *continuum* of development, but
it did not do so). Spengler's "morphology" is *biologi-
cal*, and that gives it its limitations (what does he mean
by the "senescence" and "decline" of a culture?). For
the concept of education, this means that we can neither
idealistically accept classical antiquity as *the* foundation, nor simply eliminate it, biologically and morpho-
logically, from our pattern of education. Until we can
see further into it, it will be as well to base our attitude
to the past, and to classical antiquity in particular, not
on a general concept of history, but solely on *facts* and
achievements. . . . Personally, I am afraid, I have always felt cool towards the Renaissance and classicism;

they seem to me somehow alien, and I cannot make them my own. I wonder whether a knowledge of other countries and an intimate contact with them are not more important for education today than a knowledge of the classics. In either case, of course, there is the possibility of philistinism; but perhaps one of our tasks is to see that our contacts with other peoples and countries reach out beyond politics or commerce or snobbishness to something really educational. In that way we should be tapping a hitherto unused source for the fertilizing of our education, and at the same time carrying on an old European tradition.

The wireless is just announcing the approach of strong contingents of aircraft. We could see a good deal of the last two daylight raids on Berlin; there were fairly large formations flying through a cloudless sky and leaving vapour trails behind them, and at times there was plenty of flak. The alarm was on for two and a half hours yesterday, longer than at night. Today the sky is overcast. . . . The siren is just going, so I must break off and write again later.—It lasted two hours. "Bombs were dropped in all parts of the city" says the wireless. In my time here I have been trying to observe how far people believe in anything "supernatural." Three ideas seem to be widespread, each being partly expressed in some superstitious practice: (1) Time after time one hears "Keep your fingers crossed," some sort of power being associated with the accompanying thought; people do not want to feel alone in times of danger, but to be sure of some invisible presence. (2) "Touch wood" is the exclamation every evening, when the question is discussed "whether they will come tonight or not"; this seems to be a recollection of the wrath of God on the *hubris* of man, a metaphysical, and not merely a moral reason for humility. (3) "If it's got your number on, you'll get it," and therefore everyone may as well stay where he is. On a Christian interpretation these three points might be regarded as a recollection of intercession and community, of God's wrath and grace, and of divine guidance. To the last-mentioned we might add another remark that is very often heard here: "Who knows what good may come of it?" There does not seem to me to be any trace of a recollection of eschatology. I wonder whether you have noticed anything different. . . .

This is my second Passiontide here. When people suggest in their letters . . . that I am "suffering" here, I reject the thought, for it seems to me a profanation. These things must not be dramatized. I doubt very much whether I am "suffering" any more than you, or most people, are suffering today. Of course, a great deal here is horrible, but where isn't it? Perhaps we have made too much of this question of suffering, and been too solemn about it. I have sometimes been surprised that the Roman Catholics take so little notice of that kind of thing. Is it because they are stronger than we are? Perhaps they know better from their own history what suffering and martyrdom really are, and are silent about petty inconveniences and obstacles. I believe, for instance, that physical sufferings, actual pain and so on, are certainly to be classed as "suffering." We so like to stress spiritual suffering; and yet that is just what Christ is supposed to have taken from us, and I can find nothing about it in the New Testament, or in the acts of the early martyrs. After all, whether "the Church suffers" is not at all the same as whether one of its servants has to put up with this or that. I think we need a good deal of correction on this point; indeed, I must admit candidly that I sometimes feel almost ashamed of how often we have talked about our own sufferings. No, suffering must be something quite different, and have a quite different dimension, from what I have so far experienced.

Now that's enough for today. When shall we be able

to talk together again? Keep well, enjoy the beautiful
country, spread *hilaritas* around you, and keep it yourself too! . . .

19 March 1944

With the news of the heavy fighting in your neighbourhood, you are hardly ever out of my thoughts; every
word that I read in the Bible, and every line of a hymn,
I apply to you. You must be feeling particularly homesick . . . in these dangerous days, and every letter will
only make it worse. But is it not characteristic of a
man, in contrast to an immature person, that his centre
of gravity is always where he actually is, and that the
longing for the fulfillment of his wishes cannot prevent
him from being his whole self, wherever he happens to
be? The adolescent is never wholly in one place; that
is one of his essential characteristics, else he would presumably be a dullard. There is a wholeness about the
fully grown man which enables him to face an existing
situation squarely. He may have his longings, but he
keeps them out of sight, and somehow masters them;
and the more he has to overcome in order to live fully
in the present, the more he will have the respect and
confidence of his fellows, especially the younger ones,
who are still on the road that he has already travelled.
Desires to which we cling closely can easily prevent us
from being what we ought to be be and can be; and on
the other hand, desires repeatedly mastered for the sake
of present duty make us richer. Lack of desire is poverty. Almost all the people that I find in my present
surroundings cling to their own desires, and so have no
interest in others; they no longer listen, and they are
incapable of loving their neighbour. I think that even
in this place we ought to live as if we had no wishes
and no future, and just be our true selves. It is remarkable then how others come to rely on us, confide in us,
and let us talk to them. I am writing all this to you be-

cause I think you have a big task on hand just now, and because you will be glad to think, later on, that you carried it out as well as you could. When we know that someone is in danger, we want to be sure that we know him as he really is. We can have abundant life, even though many wishes remain unfulfilled—that is what I have really been trying to say. Forgive me for putting such "considerations" before you so persistently, but I am sure you will understand that considering things takes up a large part of my life here. For the rest, I must add, as a necessary supplement to what I have just written, that I am more convinced than ever that our wishes are going to be fulfilled, and that there is no need for us to throw up the sponge.

. . . Once again I am having weeks when I don't read the Bible much; I never know quite what to do about it. I have no feeling of obligation about it, and I know, too, that after some time I shall plunge into it again voraciously. May one accept this as an entirely "natural" mental process? I am almost inclined to think so; it also happened, you know, during our *vita communis*. Of course, there is always the danger of laziness, but it would be wrong to get anxious about it; we can depend upon it that after the compass has wobbled a bit, it will point in the right direction again. Don't you agree?

It is almost a year now since we spent those last days working together. . . . I very much wonder what the future has in store for us—whether we shall be together again, perhaps in our work, or whether we shall have to be content with what has been. . . .

24 March 1944

. . . I expect the question of the baby's baptism is on your mind a good deal now, and that is mainly why I am writing to you, as I think you may be troubled by a certain "inconsistency" about it. We have sometimes urged that children should be baptized as soon as possible (as it is a question of a sacrament), even if the father cannot be present. The reasons are clear. Yet I am bound to agree that you will do well to wait. Why? I still think it is right and desirable (especially as an example to the community, and in particular for a pastor) to have one's child baptized soon, assuming that it is done with a sincere faith in the efficacy of the sacrament. At the same time, the father's wish to be present and to take part in the prayers for his child has a claim to be considered. And when I examine my own feelings, I must admit that I am chiefly influenced by the thought that God also loves the still unbaptized child who is to be baptized later. The New Testament lays down no law about infant baptism; it is a gift of grace bestowed on the Church, a gift that may be received and used in firm faith, and can thus be a striking testimony of faith for the community; but to force oneself to it without the compulsion of faith is not biblical. Regarded purely as a demonstration, infant baptism loses its justification. God will not fail to hear our prayers for the child when we ask him to send the day soon when we can bring him to the font together. As long as there is a justifiable hope that that day is not far off, I cannot believe that God is concerned about the exact date. So we can quite well wait a little and trust in God's kindly providence, and do later with a stronger faith what we should at the moment feel simply to be burdensome law. . . . So I should wait for a while (without any scruples!); we shall see our way more clearly later. I think it will be better for the actual baptism; what is more important than any purely legal performance is that it should be celebrated in the fullest possible faith.

. . . You are getting to know one of my favourite parts of the world much better than I know it myself. How I should love to sit with you in the car and see the Cecilia Metella or Hadrian's Villa. I have never been able to make much of the Pietà;[42] you must explain some time why it impresses you so much.

25 March 1944

We had another very lively time last night. The view from the roof here over the city was staggering. I have heard nothing yet about the family. Thank God my parents went to P.[43] yesterday; but there was not much doing in the West. It seems to me absurd how one cannot help hoping, when an air raid is announced, that it will be the turn of other places this time—as the saying goes, "Holy St. Florian, spare my house, set others on fire"—wanting to push off on to others what one fears for oneself: "Perhaps they will get no further than Magdeburg or Stettin this time"; how often have I heard that fervent wish expressed! Such moments make one very conscious of *natura corrupta* and *peccatum originale*, and to that extent they may be quite salutary. Incidentally, there has been a very marked increase in air activity during the last few days, and it makes one wonder whether it is not a substitute for the invasion that is not materializing.

I shall not be able to make any plans for the future before May. I am gradually losing faith in all these forecasts about dates, and I am attaching less importance to them; who knows whether it will not then be "in July?" I feel that my own personal future is of quite secondary importance compared with the general situation, though, of course, the two things are very closely connected. So I hope we shall still be able to discuss our plans for the future. . . .

I am still all right here. One gradually becomes part

---

[42] By Michelangelo, in St. Peter's.

[43] Pätzig in Neumark, an estate belonging to the parents of Maria von Wedemeyer.

of the furniture, and sometimes actually has less peace and quiet than one wants.

You are quite right about the rarity of landscape painting in the South generally. Is the south of France an exception—and Gauguin? or perhaps they were not southerners? I don't know. What about Claude Lorrain? Yet it is alive in Germany and England. The southerner has the beauties of nature, while we long for them wistfully, as for a rarity. By the way, to change the subject: Mörike once said that "where beauty is, there is happiness too." Does that not fit in with Burckhardt? We are apt to acquiesce in Nietzsche's crude alternatives, as if the only concepts of beauty were on the one hand the "Apolline" and on the other the "Dionysian," or as we should now say, the demonic. That is not so at all. Take, for example, Brueghel or Velasquez, or Hans Thoma, Leopold von Kalckreuth, or the French impressionists. There we have a beauty that is neither classical nor demonic, but simply earthly, though it has its own proper place. For myself, I must say that that is the only kind of beauty that really appeals to me. I would include the Magdeburg virgins and the Naumburg sculptures. May not the "Faustian" interpretation of Gothic art be on altogether wrong lines? How else would there be such a contrast between the plastic arts and architecture? . . .

That must be all for today, or you would never get through this letter. I am so glad to remember how you played the cantata *Lobe den Herrn* that time. It did us all a lot of good! . . .

27 March 1944

Perhaps I already ought to be sending you my special good wishes for Easter, for I don't know how long it takes for letters to reach you. . . . In looking through *Das Neue Lied* these days, I am constantly reminded that it is mainly to you that I owe my enjoyment of the Easter hymns. It is a year now since I have heard a hymn sung. But it is strange how the music that we hear inwardly can almost surpass, if we really concentrate on it, what we hear physically. It has a greater purity, the dross falls away, and in a way the music acquires a "new body." There are only a few pieces that I know well enough to be able to hear them inwardly, but I get on particularly well with the Easter hymns. I am getting a better existential appreciation of the music that Beethoven composed after he had gone deaf, in particular the great set of variations from Opus III:

By the way, I have sometimes listened lately to the Sunday evening concert from 6 to 7, though on an atrocious wireless set. . . .

Easter? We are paying more attention to dying than to death. We are more concerned to get over the act of dying than to overcome death. Socrates mastered the art of dying; Christ overcame death as "the last enemy" (I Cor. 15.26). There is a real difference between the two things; the one is within the scope of human possibilities, the other means resurrection. It is not from *ars moriendi*, the art of dying, but from the resurrection of Christ, that a new and purifying wind can blow through our present world. *Here* is the answer to δὸς μοὶ ποῦ στῶ καὶ κινήσω τὴν γῆν.[44] If a few people really believed that and acted on it in their daily lives, a great deal would be changed. To live in the light of the resurrection—that is what Easter means. Do you find, too, that most people do not know what they really live by? This *perturbatio animorum* spreads amazingly. It is an unconscious waiting for the word of deliverance, though

[44] Give me a place to stand and I will move the earth.

the time is probably not yet ripe for it to be heard. But the time will come, and this Easter may be one of our last chances to prepare ourselves for our great task of the future. I hope you will be able to enjoy it, in spite of all the hardships that you are having to bear. Goodbye; I must close now. . . .

Palm Sunday,
2 April 1944

Now that Easter seems likely to come and go without our being at home and meeting again, I am putting off hope until Whitsuntide at the latest. What do you think about it? You must be having a glorious spring just now. . . . Just fancy, I have suddenly, by an odd chance, taken up graphology again, and am enjoying it very much; I am now working through Ludwig Klages' book. But I am not going to try it on my friends and relatives; there are enough people here who are interested in it. But I am convinced of the thing's reliability. I expect you know that I was so successful at it in my student days that it became embarrassing and I gave it up. That was almost 20 years ago. Now, having, I think, gotten over the dangers of psychology, I am very interested in it again, and I should like to discuss it with you. If it gets unpleasant again, I shall drop it at once. I think it is possible that you might be very successful at it, as it needs two things, the second of which you have in much greater measure than I: sensitivity, and an acute power of observation. If you like, I will write to you again about it.

In Karl Kindt's 800-page biography of Klopstock (1941) I found some very striking extracts from the latter's play *Der Tod Adams*, which is about the death of the first man. The ode is interesting enough, and the play itself is powerful. I had sometimes thought of trying to rehabilitate Klopstock, so the book interests me very much. . . .

I have here a very detailed map of the environs of Rome; I often look at it when I am thinking of you, and imagine you going round the streets with which you are familiar from long acquaintance, hearing the sounds of war not very far away, and looking at the sea from the mountains. . . .

11 April 1944

I really intended to write to you at Easter, but I had so many well-meaning visitors that I had less peace and quiet than I should have liked. . . . I have gotten so used to the silence of solitude by now, that after a short time I long for it again. I cannot imagine myself spending the day as I used to with you, or as you do now. . . . I would certainly like to have a good talk with someone, but aimless gossip gets on my nerves terribly. . . .

How did you spend Easter? Were you in Rome? How did you get over your homesickness? I should imagine that that is more difficult in your position than in mine, for it cannot be done merely through diversion and distraction. You need to get right down to fundamentals to come to terms with life, and for that you need plenty of time to yourself. I find these first warm days of spring rather trying, and I expect you do too. When nature is rediscovering herself, and the actual communities in which we live remain in unresolved tension, we feel the discord particularly keenly. Or it may be really nothing but homesickness, which it is good for us to feel keenly. At any rate, I must say that I myself have lived for many, many years quite absorbed in aims and tasks and hopes without any personal hankerings; and perhaps that has made me old before my time. It has made everything too "matter-of-fact." Almost everyone has aims and tasks, and everything is objectified, reified to such a tremendous extent —how many people today allow themselves any strong personal feeling and real yearning, or take the trouble to spend their strength freely in working out and carrying out that yearning, and letting it bear fruit? Those sentimental radio hits, with their artificial naïveté and empty crudities, are the pitiful remains and the maximum that people will tolerate by way of mental effort; it is a ghastly desolation and impoverishment. By contrast, we can be very glad when something affects us deeply, and regard the accompanying pains as an enrichment. High tensions produce big sparks (is that not a physical fact? If it is not, then translate it into the right kind of language). I have long had a special affection for the season between Easter and Ascension Day. Here is another great tension. How can people stand earthly tensions if they know nothing of the tension between heaven and earth? Have you by chance a copy of *Das Neue Lied* with you? I well remember learning the Ascension hymns with you, among them the one that I am fondest of today: *Auf diesen Tag bedenken wir.* . . . Just about now, by the way, we are beginning the tenth year of our friendship; that is a fairly large slice of one's life, and in the past year we have shared things together almost as closely as in the previous years of our *vita communis.*

. . . I have a feeling that when we two—you and I—get back home, it will be at the same time. I have been told that I had better not, for the time being, expect any change in my present position—and that is after they have been giving me fresh promises every fortnight. I don't think that is either right or clever, and I have my own ideas about it; I should very much like to tell them to you, but as I cannot have my own way, I must just make the best of it, and go on hoping for Whitsuntide.

I heard someone say yesterday that the last years had been completely wasted as far as he was concerned. I am very glad that I have never yet had that feeling, even for a moment. Nor have I ever regretted my decision in the summer of 1939,[45] for I am firmly convinced—however strange it may seem—that my life has followed a straight and unbroken course, at any rate in its outward conduct. It has been an uninterrupted enrichment of experience, for which I can only be thankful. If I were to end my life here in these conditions, that would have a meaning that I think I could understand; on the other hand, everything might be a thorough preparation for a new start and a new task when peace comes. . . .

Now I will close for today; I have another graphological analysis to make. That is how I am passing the time when I cannot do any serious work. This letter is rather disjointed owing to repeated interruptions while I was writing it. . . .

22 April 1944

. . . When you say that my time here will be very important for my practical work, and that you are very much looking forward to what I shall have to tell you later, and to what I have written, you must not indulge in any illusions about me. I certainly learnt a great deal, but I don't think I have changed very much. There are people who change, and others who can hardly change at all. I don't think I have ever changed very much, except perhaps at the time of my first impressions abroad and under the first conscious influence of Father's personality. It was then that I turned from phraseology to reality. I don't think, in fact, that you yourself have changed much. Self-development is, of course, a different matter. Neither of us has really had a break in our lives. Of course, we have deliberately broken with a good deal, but that again is something quite different. Even our present experiences probably do not represent a break in the passive sense. I some-

[45] See p. xix.

times used to long for something of the kind, but today
I think differently about it. Continuity with one's own
past is a great gift, too. Paul wrote II Tim. 1.3 as well
as I Tim. 1.13. I am often surprised how little (in contrast to nearly all the others here) I grub among my
past mistakes and think how different one thing or another would be today if I had acted differently in the
past; it does not worry me at all. Everything seems to
have taken its natural course, and to be determined
necessarily and straightforwardly by a higher providence. Do you feel the same?

I have often wondered lately why we grow insensitive to hardships in the course of time. When I think
how I felt for weeks a year ago, it strikes me very much.
I now see the same things quite differently. To put it
down to nature's self-protection does not seem to me
adequate; I am more inclined to think that it may come
from a clearer and more sober estimate of our own
limitations and possibilities, which makes it possible
for us genuinely to love our neighbour; as long as we
let our imagination run riot, love of one's neighbour
remains something vague and abstract. Today I can
take a calmer view of other people, their predicaments
and needs, and so I am better able to help them. I
would speak of clarification rather than of insensitive-
ness; but of course, we are always having to try to
change one into the other. I do not think we need reproach ourselves just because our feelings grow cooler
and calmer in the course of time, though, of course,
we must always be alive to the danger of not seeing
the wood for the trees and keep a warm heart as well
as a cool head. Will these thoughts be of any use to
you?

I wonder why it is that we find some days so much
more oppressive than others, for no apparent reason.
Is it growing pains—or spiritual trial? Once they are
over, the world looks quite a different place again.

The other day I heard the angel scene from *Palestrina*[46] on the wireless, and thought of Munich. Even then, that was the only part that I specially liked. There is a great *Palestrina* fan here who cannot understand why I did not specially care for it, and he was quite thrilled when I enjoyed the angel scene.

After a rather long unproductive period, I feel in better form for work now that spring is coming. I will tell you something about it next time. Meanwhile keep well and be of good cheer. I hope that in spite of everything we shall soon have the joy of meeting again.

30 April 1944

Another month gone. Does time fly as fast with you as it does with me here? I am often surprised at it myself —and when will the month come when . . . we two can meet again? I have such a strong feeling that great events are moving the world every day and could change all our personal relationships, that I should like to write to you much oftener, partly because I don't know how much longer I shall be able to, and even more because we want to share everything with each other as often and as long as we can. I am firmly convinced that, by the time you get this letter, great decisions will already be setting things moving on all fronts. During the coming weeks we shall have to keep a stout heart, and that is what I wish you. We shall have to keep all our wits about us, so as to let nothing scare us. In view of what is coming, I am almost inclined to quote the biblical δΣί . . ., and I feel that I "long to look," like the angels in I Peter 1.12, to see how God is going to solve the apparently insoluble. I think God is about to accomplish something that, even if we take part in it either outwardly or inwardly, we can only receive with the greatest wonder and awe. Somehow it will be clear—for those who have eyes to see—that

46 By Pfitzner.

Ps. 58.11b and Ps. 9.19f. are true; and we shall have to repeat Jer. 45.5 to ourselves every day. It is harder for you to go through this . . . all alone than it is for me, so I will think of you especially, as I am already doing now.

How good it would seem to me, for both of us, if we could go through this time together, helping each other. But it is probably "better" for it not to be so, but for each of us to have to go through it alone. I find it hard not to be able to help you in anything—except by thinking of you every morning and evening when I read the Bible, and often during the day as well. You have no need to worry about me at all, for I am getting on uncommonly well—you would be surprised, if you came to see me. People here keep on telling me (as you can see, I feel very flattered by it) that I am "radiating so much peace around me," and that I am "always so cheerful,"—so that the feelings that I sometimes have to the contrary must, I suppose, rest on an illusion (not that I really believe that at all!). You would be surprised, and perhaps even worried, by my theological thoughts and the conclusions that they lead to; and this is where I miss you most of all, because I don't know whom else I could so well discuss them with, so as to have my thinking clarified. What is bothering me incessantly is the question what Christianity really is, or indeed who Christ really is, for us today. The time when people could be told everything by means of words, whether theological or pious, is over, and so is the time of inwardness and conscience —and that means the time of religion in general. We are moving towards a completely religionless time; people as they are now simply cannot be religious any more. Even those who honestly describe themselves as "religious" do not in the least act up to it, and so they presumably mean something quite different by "religious." Our whole nineteen-hundred-year-old Christian preaching and theology rest on the "religious *a priori*" of mankind. "Christianity" has always been a form—perhaps the true form—of "religion." But if one day it becomes clear that this *a priori* does not exist at all, but was a historically conditioned and transient form of human self-expression, and if therefore man becomes radically religionless—and I think that that is already more or less the case (how else is it, for example, that this war, in contrast to all previous ones, is not calling forth any "religious" reaction?)—what does that mean for "Christianity?"

It means that the foundation is taken away from the whole of what has up to now been our "Christianity," and that there remain only a few "last survivors of the age of chivalry," or a few intellectually dishonest people, on whom we can descend as "religious." Are they to be the chosen few? Is it on this dubious group of people that we are to pounce in fervour, pique, or indignation, in order to sell them our goods? Are we to fall upon a few unfortunate people in their hour of need and exercise a sort of religious compulsion on them?

If we do not want to do all that, if our final judgment must be that the western form of Christianity, too, was only a preliminary stage to a complete absence of religion, what kind of situation emerges for us, for the Church? How can Christ become the Lord of the religionless as well? Are there religionless Christians? If religion is only a garment of Christianity—and even this garment has looked very different at different times —then what is a religionless Christianity? Barth, who is the only one to have started along this line of thought, did not carry it to completion, but arrived at a positivism of revelation, which in the last analysis is essentially a restoration. For the religionless working man (or any other man) nothing decisive is gained here. The questions to be answered would surely be: What do a church, a community, a sermon, a liturgy, a Christian life mean in a religionless world? How do we speak of God—without religion, i.e. without the temporally conditioned presuppositions of metaphysics, inwardness, and so on? How do we speak (or perhaps we cannot now even "speak" as we used to) in a "secular" way about "God?" In what way are we "religionless-secular" Christians, in what way are we the ἐκκλησία, those who are called forth, not regarding ourselves from a religious point of view as specially favoured, but rather as belonging wholly to the world? In that case Christ is no longer an object of religion, but something quite different, really the Lord of the world. But what does that mean? What is the place of worship and prayer in a religionless situation? Does the secret discipline, or alternatively the difference (which I have suggested to you before) between penultimate and ultimate take on a new importance here?

I must break off for today, so that the letter can be posted straight away. I will write to you again about it in two days' time. I hope you see more or less what I mean, and that it does not bore you. Good-bye for the present. It is not easy always to write without an echo, and you must excuse me if that makes it something of a monologue.

I find, after all, that I can write a little more.—The Pauline question whether περιτομή [circumcision] is a condition of justification seems to me in present-day terms to be whether religion is a condition of salvation. Freedom from περιτομή is also freedom from religion. I often ask myself why a "Christian instinct" often draws me more to the religionless people than to the religious, by which I do not in the least mean with any evangelizing intention, but, I might almost say, "in brotherhood." While I am often reluctant to mention God by name to religious people—because that name somehow seems to me here not to ring true, and I feel myself to be slightly dishonest (it is particularly bad when others start to talk in religious jargon; I then dry up almost completely and feel awkward and uncomfortable)—to people with no religion I can on occasion mention him by name quite calmly and as a matter of course. Religious people speak of God when human knowledge (perhaps simply because they are too lazy to think) has come to an end, or when human resources fail— in fact it is always the *deus ex machina* that they bring on to the scene, either for the apparent solution of insoluble problems, or as strength in human failure—always, that is to say, exploiting human weakness or human boundaries. Of necessity, that can go on only till people can by their own strength push these boundaries somewhat further out, so that God becomes superfluous as a *deus ex machina*. I have come to be doubtful of talking about any human boundaries (is even death, which people now hardly fear, and is sin, which they now hardly understand, still a genuine boundary today?). It always seems to me that we are trying anxiously in this way to reserve some space for God; I should like to speak of God not on the boundaries but at the centre, not in weakness but in strength; and therefore not in death and guilt but in man's life and goodness. As to the boundaries, it seems to me better to be silent and leave the insoluble unsolved. Belief in the resurrection is *not* the "solution" of the problem of death. God's "beyond" is not the beyond of our cognitive faculties. The transcendence of epistemological theory has nothing to do with the transcendence of God. God is beyond in the midst of our life. The church stands, not at the boundaries where human powers give out, but in the middle of the village. That is how it is in the Old Testament, and in this sense we still read the New Testament far too little in the light of the Old. How this religionless Christianity looks, what form it takes, is something that I am thinking about a great deal, and I shall be writing to you again about it soon. It may be that on us in particular, midway between East and West, there will fall a heavy responsibility.

Now I really must stop. It would be fine to have a word from you about all this; it would mean a great deal to me—probably more than you can imagine. Some time, just read Prov. 22.11, 12; there is something that will bar the way to any escapism disguised as piety.

5 May 1944

I suppose you must be about due for leave by now . . . and although I hope my letter will be sent on to you (and so be out-of-date), everything is so uncertain nowadays—and long experience suggests that everything is more likely to remain as it is than to change soon—that I will write to you again all the same. . . . I am getting along quite well, and so is the case, but the question of the date is still quite open. But all good things come overnight, and I am waiting and hoping confidently. . . .

A few more words about "religionlessness." I expect you remember Bultmann's essay on the "demythologizing" of the New Testament? My view of it today would be, not that he went "too far," as most people thought, but that he did not go far enough. It is not only the "mythological" concepts, such as miracle, ascension, and so on (which are not in principle separable from the concepts of God, faith, etc.), but "religious" concepts generally, which are problematic. You cannot, as Bultmann supposes, separate God and miracle, but you must be able to interpret and proclaim *both* in a "non-religious" sense. Bultmann's approach is fundamentally still a liberal one (i.e. abridging the gospel), whereas I am trying to think theologically.

What does it mean to "interpret in a religious sense?" I think it means to speak on the one hand metaphysically, and on the other hand individualistically. Neither of these is relevant to the Bible message or to the man of today. Has not the individualistic question about personal salvation almost completely left us all? Are we not really under the impression that there are more important things than that question (perhaps not more important than the *matter* itself, but more important than the *question*!)? I know it sounds pretty monstrous to say that. But, fundamentally, is it not actually biblical? Does the question about saving one's soul appear in the Old Testament at all? Are not righteousness and the Kingdom of God on earth the focus of everything, and is it not true that Rom. 3.24ff. is not an individualistic doctrine of salvation, but the culmination of the view that God alone is righteous? It is not with the beyond that we are concerned, but with this world as created and preserved, subjected to laws, reconciled, and restored. What is above this world is, in the gospel, intended to exist *for* this world; I mean that, not in the anthropocentric sense of liberal, mystic, pietistic, ethical theology, but in the biblical sense of the creation and of the incarnation, crucifixion, and resurrection of Jesus Christ.

Barth was the first theologian to begin the criticism of religion, and that remains his really great merit; but he put in its place a positivist doctrine of revelation which says, in effect, "Like it or lump it": virgin birth, Trinity, or anything else; each is an equally significant and necessary part of the whole, which must simply be swallowed as a whole or not at all. That is not biblical. There are degrees of knowledge and degrees of significance; that means that a secret discipline must be restored whereby the *mysteries* of the Christian faith are protected against profanation. The positivism of revelation makes it too easy for itself, by setting up, as it does in the last analysis, a law of faith, and so mutilates what is—by Christ's incarnation!—a gift for us. In the place of religion there now stands the Church—that is in itself biblical—but the world is in some degree made to depend on itself and left to its own devices, and that is the mistake.

I am thinking about how we can reinterpret in a "worldly" sense—in the sense of the Old Testament and of John 1.14—The concepts of repentance, faith, justification, rebirth, and sanctification. I shall be writing to you about it again.

Forgive me for writing all this in German script; normally I do this only when my writing is for my own use—and perhaps what I have written was more to clear my own mind than to edify you. I really don't want to trouble you with problems, for you may well have no time to come to grips with them, and they may only bother you; but I can't help sharing my thoughts with you, simply because that is the best way to make them clear to myself. If that does not suit you at present, please say so.—Tomorrow is Cantate,[47] and I shall be thinking of you and enjoying very pleasant memories. . . . Good-bye. Be patient, as we are, and keep well.

6 May 1944

. . . I shall be writing next time about Christians' "egoism" ("selfless self-love"). I think we agree about it. Too much altruism is oppressive and exacting; "egoism" can be less selfish and less demanding.

Cantate

I have just heard some good morning-music by Reger and Hugo Distler; it was a good beginning for Sunday. The only jarring note was an interruption announcing that "enemy air squadrons are moving towards . . ." The connection between the two is not immediately obvious.

[47] The fourth Sunday after Easter.

I thought last night about what mothers-in-law should do. . . . I am sure that they should not try to teach; what right have they to undertake anything of the kind? It is their privilege to have a *grown-up* daughter or son, and they ought to regard that as an enrichment of their family, not as an occasion for criticism. They may find joy in their children, and give them help and advice if they are asked to, but the marriage completely relieves them of any responsibility for upbringing; that is really a privilege. I believe that when a mother-in-law sees that her child is really loved . . . she should just be glad of it and let everything else take a back seat, especially any attempts to alter character!

There are few people who know how to value reticence. . . . The siren is just going; more later.—Well, it was pretty heavy again. . . .

With regard to reticence, it all depends on *what* we are keeping to ourselves, and on whether there is one person with whom we can share everything. . . . I think it would be going too far to speak of the jealousy of mothers-in-law; it would be truer to say that there are two kinds of love, a mother's and a wife's; and that gives rise to a great deal of misunderstanding. Incidentally, it is much easier for sons-in-law than for daughters-in-law to get on peacefully with a mother-in-law—although the Bible gives a unique example to the contrary in Naomi and Ruth. . . .

Just lately I have been in the city again a few times;[48] the result has been quite satisfactory. But as the question of the date is still unresolved, I am really losing interest in my case; I often quite forget it for weeks on end. That's all for now. God keep you and all of us.

9 May 1944

I am so glad to hear that you are hoping to come home on leave soon. If you can manage to have the baptism

[48] For judicial examination.

in a few days' time . . . I should not like the thought
of my absence to cast the least shadow on your happiness, and particularly on you personally. . . . I shall
try to write you something for the occasion, and you
know that I shall be with you in spirit. It is painful
to me, to be sure, that the improbable has happened,
and that I shall not be able to celebrate the day with
you; but I have quite reconciled myself to it. I believe
that nothing that happens to me is meaningless, and
that it is good for us all that it should be so, even if it
runs counter to our own wishes. As I see it, I am here
for some purpose, and I only hope I may fulfill it. In
the light of the great purpose all our privations and dis-
appointments are trivial. Nothing would be more un-
worthy and wrong-headed than to turn one of those
rare occasions of joy, such as you are now experienc-
ing, into a calamity because of my present situation.
That would go entirely against the grain, and would
undermine my optimism with regard to my case. However thankful we may be for all our personal pleasures,
we must not for a moment lose sight of the great things
that we are living for, and they must shed light rather
than gloom on your joy. I could not bear to think that
your few weeks of happiness, which you have had difficulty enough in getting, should be in the very least
clouded by my present circumstances. That would be a
real calamity, and the other is not. My only concern
is to help you, as far as I can, to keep the lustre of
these spring days . . . as radiant as may be. Please
don't think for a moment that you are missing something through my not being with you—far from it! And
above all, please don't think I am finding it difficult to
get these words out for your sake; on the contrary, they
are my most earnest request to you, and its fulfillment
would simply make me pleased and happy. If we did
manage to meet while you are on leave, I should be
only too delighted; but please don't put yourself out

over it—I still have vivid memories of 23 December! And please don't lose a single day for the sake of spending a little time with me here. I know you would willingly do so, but it would only distress me. Of course, if your father could arrange for you to visit me, as he did in December, I should be extremely grateful. Anyway, I know we shall be thinking of each other every morning as we read the *Losungen*,[49] and I am very glad you will be able to read the Bible together again morning and evening; it will be a great help to you, not only for these present days, but for the future. Don't let the shortness of your time together and the thought that you must soon part overshadow the happiness of your leave. Don't try to do too much; let other people come and see you, instead of your going round everywhere to them, and enjoy every hour of the day peacefully as a great gift. My own opinion is that the next few weeks will bring such great and surprising events that when you start your leave you will really not know how it is all going to turn out. However much these events may affect our own personal destinies, I do hope they will not rob either of you of the peace and quietness that you need during your time together. It is a good thing that you have the chance of meeting now and deciding on all your plans together.

How I should have loved to baptize your little boy; but that is of no great consequence. Above all, I hope the baptism will help to assure you that your own lives, as well as the child's, are in safe keeping, and that you can face the future with confidence. Are you going to choose the text for the baptism yourself? If you are still looking for one, what about II Tim. 2.1, or Prov. 23.26 or 4.18? (I only came across the last of these recently; I think it is beautiful.)

I don't want to bother you with too long a letter just

[49] See p. 100, n. 26.

at the beginning of your reunion; all I wanted to do
was to send you my good wishes and tell you that I am
sharing your pleasure. Mind you have plenty of good
music!

16 May 1944

I have just heard that you have sent a message saying
that you hope to arrive this morning. You can't imagine
how glad and relieved I am that you can be here just
now. For once I could almost talk about "providence,"
and an "answer to prayer"; and perhaps you feel the
same. . . . I'm still writing something for the baptism.
What would you think of Ps. 90.14 as a text? I might
have suggested Isa. 8.18, but I thought it was rather
too general.

18 May 1944

I very much wanted to write you something for the
day of the baptism. . . . I am sending it just to show
you that I am thinking very much about you. . . . I
hope you will always have specially happy memories
of this day, and that it will give your short time together that essential quality that will endure across the
time of your separation (which I trust will be brief).
Some memories are painful, and others strengthen one;
this day will strengthen you. . . . Please harbour no
regrets about me. Martin [Niemöller] has had nearly
seven years of it, and that is a very different matter.
. . . I have just heard the great news that I am likely
to see you here tomorrow—I had given up hoping for
it. So I am spending today getting ready for your visit.
Who managed to arrange it? Whoever it was, I am most
grateful to him.

19 May 1944

I cannot tell you how delighted I was with your visit;
and your courage in deciding to come in, just the two

of you together, was splendid. . . . I am deeply moved
by what you told me about your recent experiences. I
am in too great a hurry to go into details today. Above
all, I hope you will find the peace, both within and
without, that you need after your upsetting experiences.
I am so sorry that the alarm was on just when you
came, and I breathed a sigh of relief when the commandant brought your telephone message. The question
of the "meaning" of things is often burdensome; but
don't you think it is very important that we at least
know *why* all this is necessary and has to be endured,
although the "what for" is problematical; that is clearer
for me here.

20 May 1944

. . . There is always the danger that intense love may
cause one to lose what I might call the polyphony of
life. What I mean is that God wants us to love him
eternally with our whole hearts—not in such a way as
to injure or weaken our earthly love, but to provide a
kind of *cantus firmus* to which the other melodies of
life provide the counterpoint. One of these contrapuntal
themes (which have their own complete independence
but are yet related to the *cantus firmus*) is earthly affection. Even in the Bible we have the Song of Songs;
and really one can imagine no more ardent, passionate,
sensual love than is portrayed there (see 7.6). It is a
good thing that that book is in the Bible, in face of all
those who believe that the restraint of passion is Christian (where is there such restraint in the Old Testament?). Where the *cantus firmus* is clear and plain, the
counterpoint can be developed to its limits. The two
are "undivided and yet distinct," in the words of the
Chalcedonian Definition, like Christ in his divine and
human natures. May not the attraction and importance
of polyphony in music consist in its being a musical reflection of this Christological fact and therefore of our

vita christiana? This thought did not occur to me till after your visit yesterday. Do you see what I am driving at? I wanted to tell you to have a good, clear *cantus firmus*; that is the only way to a full and perfect sound, when the counterpoint has a firm support and cannot come adrift or get out of tune, while remaining a distinct whole in its own right. Only a polyphony of this kind can give life a wholeness and at the same time assure us that nothing calamitous can happen as long as the *cantus firmus* is kept going. Perhaps a good deal will be easier to bear in these days together, and possibly also in the days ahead when you are separated. Please . . . do not fear and hate the separation, if it should come again with all its dangers, but rely on the *cantus firmus*.—I don't know whether I have made myself clear now, but one so seldom speaks of such things. . . .

21 May 1944

I have just written the date of this letter as my share in the baptism and the preparations for it. At the same moment the siren went, and now I am sitting in the sick-bay and hoping that today at any rate you will have no air raid. What times these are! What a baptism! And what memories for the years to come! What matters is that we should direct these memories, as it were, into the right spiritual channels, and so make them harder, clearer, and more defiant, which is a good thing. There is no place for sentimentality on a day like this. If in the middle of an air raid God sends out the gospel call to his kingdom in baptism, it will be quite clear what that kingdom is and what it means. It is a kingdom stronger than war and danger, a kingdom of power and authority, signifying eternal terror and judgment to some, and eternal joy and righteousness to others, not a kingdom of the heart, but one as wide as the earth, not transitory but eternal, a kingdom that makes a way for itself and summons men to itself to prepare its way, a kingdom for which it is worth while to risk our lives.—

The shooting is just beginning, but it does not seem likely to be very bad today. I should so like to hear you preaching in a few hours' time. . . . At eight this morning I heard a chorale prelude on *Was Gott tut, das ist wohlgetan*—a good beginning to the day; as I listened to it, I thought of you. . . . I had heard no organ for a long time, and the sound of it was like a refuge in time of trouble. . . .

I suppose you will have to make an after-dinner speech today, and that you will be thinking of me as you do so. I should very much like to hear what you said. The very fact that we so rarely say such words to one another makes one long for them from time to time. Do you understand that? Perhaps one feels it all the more strongly through being here cut off from other people. I used to take such things for granted, and in fact I still do, in spite of everything. . . .

The image of polyphony is still pursuing me. When I was rather distressed today at not being with you, I could not help thinking that pain and joy are also part of life's polyphony, and that they can exist independently side by side. . . .

All clear. I am glad for your sake.—I have on my desk two wonderful sprigs of lilac, which a kind man brought for me. The photographs that you brought I have put in front of me, and I am looking at the baby who is being baptized today. . . . I think he is lovely, and if he is to take after me at all physically, I only hope he will have my freedom from toothache and headache, and my leg muscles and sensitive palate (though the latter is not an unmixed blessing). For other things he can do better elsewhere. . . . He has also inherited the best thing about me, my name. I have always been satisfied with it, and as a boy I was actually proud of it. Believe me, I shall always be a good godfather to him and do all I possibly can to help him. I don't think he could choose a better one! . . .

If war sometimes seems to you to mean nothing but death, you are probably not doing justice to the manifold ways of God. We all have our appointed hour of death, and it will find us wherever we go. And we must be ready for it. But

> *Er weiss viel tausend Weisen,*
> *zu retten aus dem Tod,*
> *ernährt und gibet Speisen*
> *zur Zeit der Hungersnot.*[50]

That is something we must not forget.—Another alarm. . . . I am sending you a letter to give to Niebuhr, in case of need.[51] Also in case of need, we must arrange a rendezvous. Later on I expect we shall be able to keep in touch through N. and Uncle George.[52]

THOUGHTS ON THE BAPTISM OF D.W.R.[53]

May 1944

You are the first of a new generation in our family, and therefore the oldest representative of your generation. You will have the priceless advantage of spending a good part of your life with the third and fourth generation that went before you. Your great-grandfather will be able to tell you, from his own personal memories, of people who were born in the eighteenth century; and one day, long after the year 2000, you will be the living bridge over which your descendants will get an oral

---

[50] "He knows thousands of ways to save us from death; he nourishes us and gives us food in time of famine" (from *Du meine Seele, singe* by Paul Gerhardt).

[51] I.e. in case of becoming a prisoner-of-war.

[52] Dr. G. K. A. Bell, Bishop of Chichester.

[53] Dietrich Wilhelm Rüdiger Bethge.

tradition of more than 250 years—all this *sub condi-tione Jacobea*, "if the Lord wills."[54] So your birth provides us with a suitable occasion to reflect on the changes that time brings, and to try to scan the outlines of the future.

🏵   🏵   🏵

The three names that you bear refer to three houses with which your life is, and always should be, inseparably connected. Your grandfather on your father's side lived in a country parsonage. A simple, healthy life, with wide intellectual interests, joy in the most homely things, a natural and unaffected interest in ordinary people and their work, a capacity for self-help in practical things, and a modesty grounded in spiritual contentment—those are the earthly values which were at home in the country parsonage, and which you will meet in your father. In all the circumstances of life you will find them a firm basis for living together with other people, and for achieving real success and inward happiness.

The urban middle-class culture embodied in the home of your mother's parents has led to pride in public service, intellectual achievement and leadership, and a deep-rooted sense of duty towards a great heritage and cultural tradition. This will give you, even before you are aware of it, a way of thinking and acting which you can never lose without being untrue to yourself.

It was a kindly thought of your parents that you should be known by the name of your great-uncle, who is a pastor and a great friend of your father's; he is at present sharing the fate of many other good Germans and Protestant Christians, and so he has only been able to participate at a distance in your parents' wedding and in your own birth and baptism, but he looks for-

[54] James 4.15.

ward to your future with great confidence and cheerful
hope. He is striving to keep up the spirit—as far as he
understands it—that is embodied in his parents' (your
great-grandparents') home. He takes it as a good omen
for your future that it was in that home that your parents got to know each other, and he hopes that one
day you will be thankful for its spirit and draw on the
strength that it gives.

By the time you have grown up, the old country parsonage and the old town villa will belong to a vanished
world. But the old spirit, after a time of misunderstanding and weakness, withdrawal and recovery, preservation and rehabilitation, will produce new forms.
To be deeply rooted in the soil of the past makes life
harder, but it also makes it richer and more vigorous.
There are in human life certain fundamental truths to
which men will always return sooner or later. So there
is no need to hurry; we have to be able to wait. "God
seeks what has been driven away" (Eccles. 3.15).

  ❊ ❊ ❊

In the revolutionary times ahead the greatest gift will
be to know the security of a good home. It will be a
bulwark against all dangers from within and without.
The time when children broke away in arrogance from
their parents will be past. Children will be drawn into
their parents' protection, and they will seek refuge,
counsel, peace, and enlightenment. You are lucky to
have parents who know at first hand what it means to
have a parental home in stormy times. In the general
impoverishment of intellectual life you will find your
parents' home a storehouse of spiritual values and a
source of intellectual stimulation. Music, as your parents understand and practise it, will help to dissolve
your perplexities and purify your character and sensi-
bility, and in times of care and sorrow will keep a
ground-bass of joy alive in you. Your parents will soon

be teaching you to help yourself and never to be afraid of soiling your hands. The piety of your home will not be noisy or loquacious, but it will teach you to say your prayers, to fear and love God above everything, and to do the will of Jesus Christ. "My son, keep your father's commandment, and forsake not your mother's teaching. Bind them upon your heart always; tie them about your neck. When you walk, they will lead you; when you lie down, they will watch over you; and when you awake, they will talk with you" (Prov. 6.20–22). "Today salvation has come to this house" (Luke 19.9).

※　※　※

I wish you could grow up in the country; but it will not be the countryside in which your father grew up. People used to think that the big cities offered the fullest kind of life and lots of pleasure, and they used to flock to them as though to a festival; but those cities have now brought on themselves death and dying, with all imaginable horrors, and have become fearsome places from which women and children have fled. The age of big cities on our continent seems to have come to an end. According the Bible, Cain founded the first city. It may be that a few world metropolises will survive, but their brilliance, however alluring it may be, will in any case have something uncanny about it for a European. On the other hand, the flight from the cities will mean that the countryside is completely changed. The peace and seclusion of country life have already been largely undermined by the radio, the car, and the telephone, and by the spread of bureaucracy into almost every department of life; and now if millions of people who can no longer endure the pace and the demands of the city are moving into the country, and if entire industries are dispersed into rural areas, then the urbanization of the country will go ahead fast, and the whole basic structure of life there will be changed.

The village of thirty years ago no more exists today
than the idyllic South Sea island. In spite of man's
longing for peace and solitude, these will be difficult
to find. But with all these changes, it will be an advantage to have under one's feet a plot of land from
which to draw the resources of a new, natural, un-
pretentious, and contented day's work and evening's
leisure. "There is great gain in godliness and contentment; . . . if we have food and clothing, with these
we shall be content" (I Tim. 6.6f.). "Give me neither
poverty nor riches; feed me with the food that is need-
ful for me, lest I be full, and deny thee, and say, 'Who
is the Lord?', or lest I be poor, and steal, and profane
the name of my God" (Prov. 30.8f.). "Flee from the
midst of Babylon. . . . She was not healed. . . . Forsake her, and let us go each to his own country" (Jer.
51.6, 9).

※　　※　　※

We have grown up with the experience of our parents and grandparents that a man can and must plan,
develop, and shape his own life, and that life has a
purpose, about which a man must make up his mind,
and which he must then pursue with all his strength.
But we have learnt by experience that we cannot plan
even for the coming day, that what we have built up
is being destroyed overnight, and that our life, in contrast to that of our parents, has become formless or
even fragmentary. In spite of that, I can only say that
I have no wish to live in any other time than our own,
even though it is so inconsiderate of our outward well-
being. We realize more clearly than formerly that the
world lies under the wrath and grace of God. We read
in Jer. 45: "Thus says the Lord: Behold, what I have
built I am breaking down, and what I have planted I
am plucking up. . . . And do you seek great things
for yourself? Seek them not; for, behold, I am bringing

evil upon all flesh; . . . but I will give your life as a prize of war in all places to which you may go." If we can save our souls unscathed out of the wreckage of our material possessions, let us be satisfied with that. If the Creator destroys his own handiwork, what right have we to lament the destruction of ours? It will be the task of our generation, not to "seek great things," but to save and preserve our souls out of the chaos, and to realize that it is the only thing we can carry as a "prize" from the burning building. "Keep your heart with all vigilance; for from it flow the springs of life" (Prov. 4.23). We shall have to keep our lives rather than shape them, to hope rather than plan, to hold out rather than march forward. But we do want to preserve for you, the rising generation, what will make it possible for you to plan, build up, and shape a new and better life.

❉   ❉   ❉

We have spent too much time in thinking, supposing that if we weigh in advance the possibilities of any action, it will happen automatically. We have learnt, rather too late, that action comes, not from thought, but from a readiness for responsibility. For you thought and action will enter on a new relationship; your thinking will be confined to your responsibilities in action. With us thought was often the luxury of the onlooker; with you it will be entirely subordinated to action. "Not every one who says to me, 'Lord, Lord,' shall enter the kingdom of heaven, but he who *does* the will of my Father who is in heaven," said Jesus (Matt. 7.21).

❉   ❉   ❉

For the greater part of our lives pain was a stranger to us. To be as free as possible from pain was unconsciously one of our guiding principles. Niceties of feeling, sensitivity to our own and other people's pain are at once the strength and the weakness of our way of life. From its early days your generation will be tougher and closer to real life, for you will have had to endure privation and pain, and your patience will have been greatly tried. "It is good for a man that he bear the yoke in his youth" (Lam. 3.27).

❀ ❀ ❀

We thought we could make our way in life with reason and justice, and when both failed, we felt that we were at the end of our tether. We have constantly exaggerated the importance of reason and justice in the course of history. You, who are growing up in a world war which ninety per cent of mankind did not want, but for which they have to risk losing their goods and their lives, are learning from childhood that the world is controlled by forces against which reason can do nothing; and so you will be able to cope with those forces more successfully. In our lives the "enemy" did not really exist. You know that you have enemies and friends, and you know what they can mean in your life. You are learning very early in life ways (which we did not know) of fighting an enemy, and also the value of unreserved trust in a friend. "Has not man a hard service upon earth?" (Job 7.1). "Blessed be the Lord, my rock, who trains my hands for war, and my fingers for battle; my rock and my fortress, my stronghold and my deliverer, my shield and he in whom I take refuge" (Ps. 144.1f.). "There is a friend who sticks closer than a brother" (Prov. 18.24).

❀ ❀ ❀

Are we moving towards an age of colossal organizations and collective institutions, or will the desire of innumerable people for small, manageable, personal relationships be satisfied? Must they be mutually exclu-

sive? Might it not be that world organizations themselves, with their wide meshes, will allow more scope
for personal interests? Similarly with the question
whether we are moving towards an age of the selection
of the fittest, i.e. an aristocratic society, or to uniformity
in all material and spiritual aspects of human life. Although there has been a very far-reaching equalization
here, the sensitiveness in all ranks of society for the
human values of justice, achievement, and courage
could create a new selection of people who will be allowed the right to provide strong leadership. It will not
be difficult for us to renounce our privileges, recogniz-
ing the justice of history. We may have to face events
and changes that take no account of our wishes and
our rights. But if so, we shall not give way to embit-
tered and barren pride, but consciously submit to divine judgment, and so prove ourselves worthy to survive
by identifying ourselves generously and unselfishly with
the life of the community and the sufferings of our fellow-men. "But any nation which will bring its neck
under the yoke of the king of Babylon and serve him,
I will leave on its own land, to till it and dwell there,
says the Lord" (Jer. 27.11). "Seek the welfare of the
city . . . and pray to the Lord on its behalf" (Jer.
29.7). "Come, my people, enter your chambers, and
shut your doors behind you; hide yourselves for a little
while until the wrath is past" (Isa. 26.20). "For his
anger is but for a moment, and his favour is for a lifetime. Weeping may tarry for the night, but joy comes
with the morning" (Ps. 30.5).

※   ※   ※

Today you will be baptized a Christian. All those
great ancient words of the Christian proclamation will
be spoken over you, and the command of Jesus Christ
to baptize will be carried out on you, without your

knowing anything about it. But we are once again being driven right back to the beginnings of our understanding. Reconciliation and redemption, regeneration and the Holy Ghost, love of our enemies, cross and resurrection, life in Christ and Christian discipleship—all these things are so difficult and so remote that we hardly venture any more to speak of them. In the traditional words and acts we suspect that there may be something quite new and revolutionary, though we cannot as yet grasp or express it. That is our own fault. Our Church, which has been fighting in these years only for its self-preservation, as though that were an end in itself, is incapable of taking the word of reconciliation and redemption to mankind and the world. Our earlier words are therefore bound to lose their force and cease, and our being Christians today will be limited to two things: prayer and righteous action among men. All Christian thinking, speaking, and organizing must be born anew out of this prayer and action. By the time you have grown up, the Church's form will have changed greatly. We are not yet out of the melting-pot, and any attempt to help the Church prematurely to a new expansion of its organization will merely delay its conversion and purification. It is not for us to prophesy the day (though the day will come) when men will once more be called on to utter the word of God that the world will be changed and renewed by it. It will be a new language, perhaps quite non-religious, but liberating and redeeming—as was Jesus' language; it will shock people and yet overcome them by its power; it will be the language of a new righteousness and truth, proclaiming God's peace with men and the coming of his kingdom. "They shall fear and tremble because of all the good and all the prosperity I provide for it" (Jer. 33.9). Till then the Christian cause will be a silent and hidden affair, but there will be those who pray and do right and wait for God's own time. May you be one of them, and may it be said of you one day, "The path of the righteous is like the light of dawn, which shines brighter and brighter till full day" (Prov. 4.18).

24 May 1944

. . . On the duties of godparents: in the old books the godparents often played a special part in a child's life. Growing children often want sympathy, kindness, and advice from grown-up people other than their parents; and the godparents are the people chosen by the parents to help in this way. The godparent has the right to give good advice, whereas the parents give orders.

. . . You need days whose memory is not painful because of something that was lacking, but a source of strength because of something that endures. I have been trying to write you a few words on the *Losungen*[55]— in fact, I was at it today while the alarm was on, and so they are rather inadequate, and not as well thought out as I could wish. . . .

I am reading with great interest Weizsäcker's book about the "world-view of physics," and I hope to learn a great deal from it for my own work. If only one had the chance to exchange ideas. . . .

25 May 1944

I hope that, in spite of the alarms, you are enjoying to the full the peace and beauty of these warm, summer-like Whitsuntide days. One gradually learns to acquire an inner detachment from life's menaces—although "acquire detachment" seems too negative, formal, artificial, and stoical; and it is perhaps more accurate to say that we assimilate these menaces into our life as a

[55] See p. 100, n. 26.

whole. I notice repeatedly here how few people there are who can harbour conflicting emotions at the same time. When bombers come, they are all fear; when there is something nice to eat, they are all greed; when they are disappointed, they are all despair; when they are successful, they can think of nothing else. They miss the fulness of life and the wholeness of an independent existence; everything objective and subjective is dissolved for them into fragments. By contrast, Christianity puts us into many different dimensions of life at the same time; we make room in ourselves, to some extent, for God and the whole world. We rejoice with those who rejoice, and weep with those who weep; we are anxious (—I was again interrupted just then by the alarm, and am now sitting out of doors enjoying the sun—) about our life, but at the same time we must think about things much more important to us than life itself. When the alarm goes, for instance: as soon as we turn our minds from worrying about our own safety to the task of helping other people to keep calm, the situation is completely changed; life is not pushed back into a single dimension, but is kept multi-dimensional and polyphonous. What a deliverance it is to be able to *think*, and thereby remain multi-dimensional. I have almost made it a rule here, simply to tell people who are trembling under an air raid that it would be much worse for a small town. We have to get people out of their one-track minds; that is a kind of "preparation" for faith, or something that makes faith possible, although really it is only faith itself that can make possible a multi-dimensional life, and so enable us to keep this Whitsuntide too, in spite of the alarms.

At first I was a bit disconcerted, and perhaps even saddened, not to have a letter from anyone this Whitsuntide. Then I told myself that it was perhaps a good sign, as it meant that no one was worrying about me. It is a strange human characteristic that we like other people to be anxious about us—at least just a trifle anxious.

Weizsäcker's book *Das Weltbild der Physik* is still keeping me very busy. It has again brought home to me quite clearly how wrong it is to use God as a stop-gap for the incompleteness of our knowledge. If in fact the frontiers of knowledge are being pushed further and further back (and that is bound to be the case), then God is being pushed back with them, and is therefore continually in retreat. We are to find God in what we know, not in what we do not know; God wants us to realize his presence, not in unsolved problems but in those that are solved. That is true of the relationship between God and scientific knowledge, but it is also true of the wider human problems of death, suffering, and guilt. It is now possible to find, even for these questions, human answers that take no account whatever of God. In point of fact, people deal with these questions without God (it has always been so), and it is simply not true to say that only Christianity has the answers to them. As to the idea of "solving" problems, it may be that the Christian answers are just as un-convincing—or convincing—as any others. Here again, God is no stop-gap; he must be recognized at the centre of life, not when we are at the end of our resources; it is his will to be recognized in life, and not only when death comes; in health and vigour, and not only in suffering; in our activities, and not only in sin. The ground for this lies in the revelation of God in Jesus Christ. He is the centre of life, and he certainly did not "come" to answer our unsolved problems. From the centre of life certain questions, and their answers, are seen to be wholly irrelevant (I am thinking of the judgment pronounced on Job's friends). In Christ there are no "Christian problems."—Enough of this; I have just been disturbed again.

30 May 1944, evening

I am sitting alone upstairs. Everything is quiet in the building; a few birds are still singing outside, and I can even hear the cuckoo in the distance. I find these long, warm evenings, which I am now living through here for the second time, rather trying. I long to be outside, and if I were not so "reasonable," I might do something foolish. I wonder whether we have become too reasonable. When you have deliberately suppressed every desire for so long, it may have one of two bad results: either it burns you up inside, or it all gets so bottled up that one day there is a terrific explosion. It is, of course, conceivable that one may become completely selfless, and I know better than anyone else that that has not happened to me. Perhaps you will say that one ought not to suppress one's desires, and I expect you would be right. . . . So I take refuge in thinking and writing letters . . . and curb my desires as a measure of self-protection. However paradoxical it may sound, it would be more selfless if I did not need to be so afraid of my desires, and could give them free rein—but that is very difficult.—Just now I happened to hear Solveig's Song on the wireless in the sick-bay. It quite got hold of me. To wait loyally a whole lifetime —that is to triumph over the hostility of space, i.e. separation, and over time, i.e. the past. Don't you think that such loyalty is the only way to happiness, and that disloyalty leads to unhappiness?—Well, I shall go to bed now, in case we have another disturbed night. Good-bye.

2 June 1944

While you are in Italy I shall write to you about the Song of Songs. I must say I should prefer to read it as an ordinary love song, and that is probably the best

"Christological" exposition. I must think again about Eph. 5. I hope that by now you have found something about Bultmann, if it has not been lost.

5 June 1944

I should be behaving like a shy boy if I concealed from you the fact that I am making some attempts here to write poetry. Up to now I have been keeping it dark. . . . So today I am sending you a sample,[56] first, because I think it would be silly to have any secrets from you, secondly, so that you can have something you did not expect to read on your journey, and thirdly, because the subject of it is a good deal in your mind at the moment, and what I have written may be on the lines of what you are . . . already thinking. This dialogue with the past, the attempt to hold on to it and recover it, and above all, the fear of losing it, is the almost daily accompaniment of my life here; and sometimes, especially after brief visits, which are always followed by long partings, it becomes a theme with variations. To take leave of others, and to live on past memories, whether it was yesterday or last year (they soon melt into one), is my ever-recurring duty, and you yourself once wrote that saying good-bye goes very much against the grain. In this attempt of mine the crucial part is the last few lines. I am inclined to think they are too brief—what do you think? Strangely enough, they came out in rhyme of their own accord. The whole thing was composed in a few hours, and I did not try to polish it. . . . Perhaps I shall suppress these impulses in future, and use my time to better advantage; but that might well depend on your opinion. If you like, I will send you some more to look at.

[56] "The Past," see pp. 215 ff.

6 June 1944
(The Normandy Landing)

I am sending you this hurried greeting, simply because I want in some way to share the day with you yourself and with all of you. The news did not come as a surprise to me, and yet things turn out differently from what we expect. Today's *Losung und Lehrtext*[57] take us to the heart of the gospel— "redemption" is the key word to it all. Let us face the coming weeks in faith and in great assurance about the general future, and commit your way and all our ways to God. Χάρις καὶ εἰρήνη![58]

8 June 1944

. . . In some respects at least, you will have left with a lighter heart than you had feared at first. We had put off our meeting from Christmas to Easter, and then from Easter to Whitsuntide; one feast went by, and then another. But the next feast is sure to be ours; I have no doubt about that now. . . .

You now ask so many important questions on the subjects that have been occupying me lately, that I should be happy if I could answer them myself. But it is all very much in the early stages; and, as usual, I am being led on more by an instinctive feeling for questions that will arise later than by any conclusions that I have already reached about them. I will try to define my position from the historical angle.

The movement that began about the thirteenth century (I am not going to get involved in any argument about the exact date) towards the autonomy of man (in which I should include the discovery of the laws by

[57] See p. 100, n. 26. The texts referred to here are Ps. 38.5 and Eph. 1.7.
[58] "Grace and peace . . ." (Rom. 1.7 etc.)

which the world lives and deals with itself in science, social and political matters, art, ethics, and religion) has in our time reached an undoubted completion. Man has learnt to deal with himself in all questions of importance without recourse to the "working hypothesis" called "God." In questions of science, art, and ethics this has become an understood thing at which one now hardly dares to tilt. But for the last hundred years or so it has also become increasingly true of religious questions; it is becoming evident that everything gets along without "God"—and, in fact, just as well as before. As in the scientific field, so in human affairs generally, "God" is being pushed more and more out of life, losing more and more ground.

Roman Catholic and Protestant historians agree that it is in this development that the great defection from God, from Christ, is to be seen; and the more they claim and play off God and Christ against it, the more the development considers itself to be anti-Christian. The world that has become conscious of itself and the laws that govern its own existence has grown self-confident in what seems to us to be an uncanny way. False developments and failures do not make the world doubt the necessity of the course that it is taking, or of its development; they are accepted with fortitude and detachment as part of the bargain, and even an event like the present war is no exception. Christian apologetic has taken the most varied forms of opposition to this self-assurance. Efforts are made to prove to a world thus come of age that it cannot live without the tutelage of "God." Even though there has been surrender on all secular problems, there still remain the so-called "ultimate questions"—death, guilt—to which only "God" can give an answer, and because of which we need God and the Church and the pastor. So we live, in some degree, on these so-called ultimate questions of humanity. But what if one day they no longer exist as such, if they too can be answered "without God?" Of course, we now have the secularized offshoots of Christian theology, namely existentialist philosophy and the psychotherapists, who demonstrate to secure, contented, and happy mankind that it is really unhappy and desperate and simply unwilling to admit that it is in a predicament about which it knows nothing, and from which only they can rescue it. Wherever there is health, strength, security, simplicity, they sent luscious fruit to gnaw at or to lay their pernicious eggs in. They set themselves to drive people to inward despair, and then the game is in their hands. That is secularized methodism. And whom does it touch? A small number of intellectuals, of degenerates, of people who regard themselves as the most important thing in the world, and who therefore like to busy themselves with themselves. The ordinary man, who spends his everyday life at work and with his family, and of course with all kinds of diversions, is not affected. He has neither the time nor the inclination to concern himself with his existential despair, or to regard his perhaps modest share of happiness as a trial, a trouble, or a calamity.

The attack by Christian apologetic on the adulthood of the world I consider to be in the first place pointless, in the second place ignoble, and in the third place unchristian. Pointless, because it seems to me like an attempt to put a grown-up man back into adolescence, i.e. to make him dependent on things on which he is, in fact, no longer dependent, and thrusting him into problems that are, in fact, no longer problems to him. Ignoble, because it amounts to an attempt to exploit man's weakness for purposes that are alien to him and to which he has not freely assented. Unchristian, because it confuses Christ with one particular stage in man's religiousness, i.e. with a human law. More about this later.

But first, a little more about the historical position.

The question is: Christ and the world that has come of age. The weakness of liberal theology was that it conceded to the world the right to determine Christ's place in the world; in the conflict between the Church and the world it accepted the comparatively easy terms of peace that the world dictated. Its strength was that it did not try to put the clock back, and that it genuinely accepted the battle (Troeltsch), even though this ended with its defeat.

Defeat was followed by surrender, and by an attempt to make a completely fresh start based on the fundamentals of the Bible and the Reformation. Heim sought, along pietist and methodist lines, to convince the individual man that he was faced with the alternative "despair or Jesus." He gained "hearts." Althaus (carrying forward the modern and positive line with a strong confessional emphasis) tried to wring from the world a place for Lutheran teaching (ministry) and Lutheran worship, and otherwise left the world to its own devices. Tillich set out to interpret the evolution of the world (against its will) in a religious sense—to give it its shape through religion. That was very brave of him, but the world unseated him and went on by itself; he, too, sought to understand the world better than it understood itself; but it felt that it was completely misunderstood, and rejected the imputation. (Of course, the world *must* be understood better than it understands itself, but not "religiously" as the religious socialists wanted.) Barth was the first to realize the mistake that all these attempts (which were all, in fact, still sailing, though unintentionally, in the channel of liberal theology) were making in leaving clear a space for religion in the world or against the world.

He brought in against religion the God of Jesus Christ, "*pneuma* against *sarx*." That remains his greatest service (his *Epistle to the Romans*, second edition, in spite of all the neo-Kantian egg-shells). Through his

later dogmatics, he enabled the Church to effect this
distinction, in principle, all along the line. It was not in
ethics, as is often said, that he subsequently failed—his
ethical observations, as far as they exist, are just as important as his dogmatic ones—; it was that in the non-
religious interpretation of theological concepts he gave
no concrete guidance, either in dogmatics or in ethics.
There lies his limitation, and because of it his theology
of revelation has become positivist, a "positivism of
revelation," as I put it.

The Confessing Church has now largely forgotten all
about the Barthian approach, and has lapsed from positivism into conservative restoration. The important
thing about that Church is that it carries on the great
concepts of Christian theology; but it seems as if doing
this is gradually just about exhausting it. It is true that
there are in those concepts the elements of genuine
prophecy (among them two things that you mention:
the claim to truth, and mercy) and of genuine worship;
and to that extent the Confessing Church gets only attention, hearing, and rejection. But both of them remain undeveloped and remote, because there is no
interpretation of them.

Those who, like e.g. Schütz or the Oxford Group or
the Berneucheners, miss the "movement" and the
"life," are dangerous reactionaries; they are reactionary
because they go right back behind the approach of the
theology of revelation and seek for "religious" renewal.
They simply have not yet understood the problem at
all, and their talk is entirely beside the point. There is
no future for them (though the Oxford Group would
have the best chance if they were not so completely
without biblical substance).

Bultmann seems to have somehow felt Barth's limitations, but he misconstrues them in the sense of liberal
theology, and so goes off into the typical liberal process
of reduction—the "mythological" elements of Christi-

anity are dropped, and Christianity is reduced to its "essence."—My view is that the full content, including the "mythological" concepts, must be kept—the New Testament is not a mythological clothing of a universal truth; this mythology (resurrection etc.) is the thing itself—but the concepts must be interpreted in such a way as not to make religion a precondition of faith (cf. Paul and circumcision). Only in that way, I think, will liberal theology be overcome (and even Barth is still influenced by it, though negatively) and at the same time its question be genuinely taken up and answered (as is *not* the case in the Confessing Church's positivism of revelation!).

Thus the world's coming of age is no longer an occasion for polemics and apologetics, but is now really better understood than it understands itself, namely on the basis of the gospel and in the light of Christ.

Now for your question whether there is any "room" left for the Church, or whether that room has gone for good; and the other question, whether Jesus did not use men's "distress" as a point of contact with them, and whether therefore the "methodism" that I criticized earlier is not right.—9th June: I am breaking off here, and will write more tomorrow. . . .

21 June 1944

. . . Now you are somewhere looking for your unit, and I hope that when you reach it you will find some letters there to greet you—assuming that your old field post number is still correct. All I want to do today is to send you a greeting. I daren't enclose the next instalment of theological argument, or any poetry, as I don't know whether the fpn. will still get you. As soon as I hear about that, there will be some more to follow. I am very grateful for your opinion and criticism of the poem. I hardly know yet what to make of these

new children of mine, as I have no standard to judge
them by.

. . . This morning we had the worst of all the air
raids so far. For several hours my room was so dark
with the cloud of smoke that hung over the city that I
almost switched the light on. I have just heard that all
is well at home. . . .

It often seems hard to have to spend the beautiful
long summer days here for the second time; but one
just cannot choose where one has to be. So we must
keep on trying to find our way through the petty
thoughts that irritate us, to the great thoughts that
strengthen us.—I am at present reading the quite outstanding book by W. F. Otto, the classics man at
Königsberg, *Die Götter Griechenlands*. To quote from
his closing words, it is about "this world of faith, which
sprang from the wealth and depth of human existence,
not from its cares and longings." Can you understand
my finding something very attractive in this theme and
its treatment, and also—*horribile dictu*—my finding
these gods, when they are so treated, less offensive than
certain brands of Christianity? In fact, that I almost
think I could claim these gods for Christ? The book is
most helpful for my present theological reflections.

SORROW AND JOY

Sorrow and joy,
striking suddenly on our startled senses,
seem, at the first approach, all but impossible
of just distinction one from the other,
even as frost and heat at the first keen contact
burn us alike.

Joy and sorrow,
hurled from the height of heaven in meteor fashion,
flash in an arc of shining menace o'er us.

Those they touch are left
stricken amid the fragments
of their colourless, usual lives.

Imperturbable, mighty,
ruinous and compelling,
sorrow and joy
—summoned or all unsought for—
processionally enter.
Those they encounter
they transfigure, investing them
with strange gravity
and a spirit of worship.

Joy is rich in fears;
sorrow has its sweetness.
Indistinguishable from each other
they approach us from eternity,
equally potent in their power and terror.

From every quarter
mortals come hurrying,
part envious, part awe-struck,
swarming, and peering
into the portent,
where the mystery sent from above us
is transmuting into the inevitable
order of earthly human drama.

What, then, is joy? What, then, is sorrow?
Time alone can decide between them,
when the immediate poignant happening
lengthens out to continuous wearisome suffering,
when the laboured creeping moments of daylight
slowly uncover the fulness of our disaster,
sorrow's unmistakable features.

Then do most of our kind,
sated, if only by the monotony
of unrelieved unhappiness,
turn away from the drama, disillusioned,
uncompassionate.

O ye mothers and loved ones—then, ah, then
comes your hour, the hour for true devotion.
Then your hour comes, ye friends and brothers!
Loyal hearts can change the face of sorrow,
softly encircle it with love's most gentle
unearthly radiance.

LETTERS TO A FRIEND

27 June 1944

Although I have no idea whether or when the post is
reaching you, I am still writing to you under the old
field post number. Before I go on with the theological
reflections, I should prefer to wait till I hear from you;
and the same goes for the verses—especially my latest,
a rather long poem[59] about my impressions here—
which are more suitable for an evening's talk than for
a long journey by post. . . .

I am at present writing an exposition of the first three
commandments. I find No. 2 particularly difficult. The
usual interpretation of idolatry as "wealth, sensuality,
and pride" seems to me quite unbiblical. That is a piece
of moralizing. Idols are worship, and idolatry implies
that people still worship something. But we do not now
worship anything, not even idols. In that respect we
are truly nihilists.

Now for some further thoughts about the Old Testament. Unlike the other oriental religions, the faith of
the Old Testament is not a religion of redemption. It is
true that Christianity has always been regarded as a religion of redemption. But is not this a cardinal error,
which separates Christ from the Old Testament and in-
terprets him on the lines of the myths about redemption? To the objection that a crucial importance is
given in the Old Testament to redemption (from Egypt,

[59] *Nächtliche Stimmen* (Lettner Verlag, Berlin); now in *I
loved this people*, SPCK, 1966, pp. 51–59.

and later from Babylon—cf. Deutero-Isaiah) it may be answered that the redemptions referred to here are *historical*, i.e. on *this* side of death, whereas everywhere else the myths about redemption are concerned to overcome the barrier of death. Israel is delivered out of Egypt so that it may live before God as God's people on earth. The redemption myths try unhistorically to find an eternity after death. Sheol and Hades are no metaphysical constructions, but images which imply that the "past," while it still exists, has only a shadowy existence in the present.

The decisive factor is said to be that in Christianity the hope of resurrection is proclaimed, and that that means the emergence of a genuine religion of redemption, the main emphasis now being on the far side of the boundary drawn by death. But it seems to me that this is just where the mistake and the danger lie. Redemption now means redemption from cares, distress, fears, and longings, from sin and death, in a better world beyond the grave. But is this really the essential character of the proclamation of Christ in the gospels and by Paul? I should say it is not. The difference between the Christian hope of resurrection and the mythological hope is that the former sends a man back to his life on earth in a wholly new way which is even more sharply defined than it is in the Old Testament.

The Christian, unlike the devotees of the redemption myths, has no last line of escape available from earthly tasks and difficulties into the eternal, but, like Christ himself ("My God, why has thou forsaken me?"), he must drink the earthly cup to the lees, and only in his doing so is the crucified and risen Lord with him, and he crucified and risen with Christ. This world must not be prematurely written off; in this the Old and New Testaments are at one. Redemption myths arise from human boundary-experiences, but Christ takes hold of a man at the centre of his life.

You see how my thoughts are constantly revolving round the same theme. Now I must substantiate them in detail from the New Testament; that will follow later.

I read in the paper about tropical heat in Italy— you poor man! It reminds me of August 1936. Ps. 121.6!

30 June 1944

Today was a hot summer's day here, and I could enjoy the sun only with mixed feelings, as I can imagine what ordeals you are having to go through. Probably you are stuck somewhere or other, tired and up to your eyes in dust and sweat, and perhaps with no chance of washing or cooling down. I suppose you sometimes almost loathe the sun. And yet, you know, I should like to feel the full force of it again, making the skin hot and the whole body aglow, and reminding me that I am a corporeal being. I should like to be tired by the sun, instead of by books and thoughts. I should like to have it awaken my animal existence—not the kind that degrades a man, but the kind that delivers him from the stuffiness and artificiality of a purely intellectual existence and makes him purer and happier. I should like, not just to see the sun and sip at it a little, but to experience it bodily. Romantic sun-worshipping that just gets intoxicated over sunrise and sunset, while it knows something of the power of the sun, does not know it as a reality, but only as a symbol. It can never understand why people worshipped the sun as a god; to do so one needs experience, not only of light and colours, but also of heat. The hot countries, from the Mediterranean to India and Central America, have been the intellectually creative countries. The colder lands have lived on the intellectual creativeness of the others, and anything original that they have produced, namely technology, serves in the last resort the material needs of life rather

than the mind. Is that what repeatedly draws us to the
hot countries? And may not such thoughts do something to compensate for the discomforts of the heat?
But I expect you are feeling that that is all the same to
you, and that you are just longing to be out of that
hell, back to Grunewald and a glass of Berlin beer. I
remember very well how I longed to get out of Italy
in June 1923, and did not breathe freely again till I
was out on a day's ramble in pouring rain in the Black
Forest. And there was no war on then, and all I had
to do was to enjoy myself. I remember, too, how in
August 1936 you rejected in horror the idea of going
to Naples. How are you standing up to it now physically? Formerly one simply could not do without the
"espresso," and K[laus], to my youthful annoyance,
threw away a lot of money on it. Besides that, we took
a coach even for the shortest distances, and consumed
vast quantities of *granitos* and *cassatas* on the way.—I
have just had the most welcome news—that you have
written, and that you have kept your old field post number, from which I conclude that you have rejoined your
old unit. You can't think how reassuring—relatively, at
any rate—that is for me. . . .

A few hours ago Uncle Paul[60] called here to inquire
personally about my welfare. It is most comical how everyone goes about flapping his wings and—with a few
notable exceptions—tries to outdo everyone else in un-
dignified ways. It is painful, but some of them are in
such a state now that they can't help it.

Now I will try to go on with the theological reflections that I broke off not long since. I had been saying
that God is being increasingly pushed out of a world
that has come of age, out of the spheres of our knowl-

[60] General Paul van Hase, Commandant of Berlin, who was
condemned to death a few weeks later by the People's Court,
and executed.

edge and life, and that since Kant he has been relegated
to a realm beyond the world of experience.

Theology has on the one hand resisted this development with apologetics, and has taken up arms—in vain
—against Darwinism, etc. On the other hand, it has
accommodated itself to the development by restricting
God to the so-called ultimate questions as a *deux ex
machina*; that means that he becomes the answer to
life's problems, and the solution of its needs and conflicts. So if anyone has no such difficulties, or if he re-
fuses to go into these things, to allow others to pity
him, then either he cannot be open to God; or else he
must be shown that he is, in fact, deeply involved in
such problems, needs, and conflicts, without admitting
or knowing it. If that can be done—and existentialist
philosophy and psychotherapy have worked out some
quite ingenious methods in that direction—then this
man can now be claimed for God, and methodism can
celebrate its triumph. But if he cannot be brought to
see and admit that his happiness is really an evil, his
health sickness, and his vigour despair, the theologian
is at his wits' end. It is a case of having to do either
with a hardened sinner of a particularly ugly type, or
with a man of "bourgeois complacency," and the one
is as far from salvation as the other.

You see, that is the attitude that I am contending
against. When Jesus blessed sinners, they were real sinners, but Jesus did not make everyone a sinner first. He
called them away from their sin, not into their sin. It
is true that encounter with Jesus meant the reversal of
all human values. So it was in the conversion of Paul,
though in his case the encounter with Jesus preceded
the realization of sin. It is true that Jesus cared about
people on the fringe of human society, such as harlots
and tax-collectors, but never about them alone, for he
sought to care about man as such. Never did he ques-

tion a man's health, vigour, or happiness, regarded in themselves, or regard them as evil fruits; else why should he heal the sick and restore strength to the weak? Jesus claims for himself and the Kingdom of God the whole of human life in all its manifestations.

Of course I must be interrupted just now! Let me just summarize briefly what I am concerned about—how to claim for Jesus Christ a world that has come of age.

I can't write any more today, or else the letter will be kept here another week, and I don't want that to happen. So: To be continued!

Uncle Paul has been here. He had me brought downstairs at once, and stayed. . . . more than five hours! He had four bottles of *Sekt* brought—a unique event in the annals of this place—and was nicer and more generous than I should ever have expected. He probably wanted to make it clear to everyone what good terms he is on with me, and what he expects from the jittery and pedantic M.[61] Such independence, which would be quite unthinkable in a civilian, was most remarkable. By the way, he told me this story: At St. Privat a wounded ensign shouted loudly, "I am wounded; long live the king." Thereupon General von Löwenfeld, who was also wounded, said, "Be quiet, ensign; we die here in silence!"—I am curious to know what will be the effect of his visit here; I mean what people will think of it.

Well, good-bye, and forgive me for breaking off. But I think you would sooner have this than nothing at all. I hope we shall be together again early in the autumn.

1 July 1944

Seven years ago today we were at Martin's[62] together!

---

[61] See p. 45, n. 7.
[62] The day that Martin Niemöller was arrested.

8 July 1944

. . . A little while ago I wrote you a letter with some very theoretical philosophy about heat. In the last few days I have been trying it on my own body. I feel as if I were in an oven, and I am wearing only a shirt that I once brought you from Sweden, and a pair of shorts . . . and the only reason why I don't complain about it is that I can imagine how badly you must be suffering from the heat, and how frivolous my former letter must have seemed to you. So I will try to squeeze a few thoughts out of my sweating brain, and let you have them. Who knows—it may be that it will not have to be too often now, and that we shall see each other sooner than we expect. The other day I read a fine and striking remark in Euripides, in a scene of reunion after a long separation: "So then, to meet again is a god."

Now for a few more thoughts on our theme. Marshalling the biblical evidence needs more lucidity and concentration than I can command at present. Wait a few more days, till it gets cooler! I have not forgotten, either, that I owe you something about the non-religious interpretation of biblical concepts. But for today, here are a few preliminary remarks:

The displacement of God from the world, and from the public part of human life, led to the attempt to keep his place secure at least in the sphere of the "personal," the "inner," and the "private." And as every man still has a private sphere somewhere, that is where he was thought to be the most vulnerable. The secrets known to a man's valet—that is, to put it crudely, the range of his intimate life, from prayer to his sexual life —have become the hunting-ground of modern pastoral workers. In that way they resemble (though with quite different intentions) the dirtiest gutter journalists—do you remember the *Wahrheit* and the *Glocke*, which made public the most intimate details about prominent people? In the one case it is social, financial, or political blackmail, and in the other, religious blackmail. Forgive me, but I cannot put it more mildly.

From the sociological point of view this is a revolution from below, a revolt of inferiority. Just as the vulgar mind is not satisfied till it has seen some highly placed personage "in his bath," or in other embarrassing situations, so it is here. There is a kind of evil satisfaction in knowing that everyone has his failings and weak spots. In my contacts with the "outcasts" of society, its "pariahs," I have noticed repeatedly that mistrust is the dominant motive in their judgment of other people. Every action, even the most unselfish, of a person of high repute is suspected from the outset. These "outcasts" are to be found in all grades of society. In a flower-garden they grub around only for the dung on which the flowers grow. The more isolated a man's life, the more easily he falls a victim to this attitude.

There is also a parallel isolation among the clergy, in what one might call the "clerical" sniffing-around-after-people's-sins in order to catch them out. It is as if you could not know a fine house till you had found a cobweb in the furthest cellar, or as if you could not adequately appreciate a good play till you had seen how the actors behave offstage. It is the same kind of thing that you find in the novels of the last fifty years, which do not think they have depicted their characters properly till they have described them in their marriage-bed, or in films where undressing scenes are thought necessary. Anything clothed, veiled, pure, and chaste is presumed to be deceitful, disguised, and impure; people here simply show their own impurity. A basic anti-social attitude of mistrust and suspicion is the revolt of inferiority.

Regarded theologically, the error is twofold. First, it is thought that a man can be addressed as a sinner only after his weaknesses and meannesses have been spied out. Secondly, it is thought that a man's essential nature consists of his inmost and most intimate background; that is defined as his "inner life," and it is precisely in those secret human places that God is to have his domain!

On the first point it is to be said that man is certainly a sinner, but is far from being mean or common on that account. To put it rather tritely, were Goethe and Napoleon sinners because they were not always faithful husbands? It is not the sins of weakness, but the sins of strength, which matter here. It is not in the least necessary to spy out things; the Bible never does so. (Sins of strength: in the genius, *hubris*; in the peasant, the breaking of the order of life—is the decalogue a peasant ethic?—; in the bourgeois, fear of free responsibility. Is this correct?)

On the second point: the Bible does not recognize our distinction between the outward and the inward. Why should it? It is always concerned with *anthrōpos teleios*, the *whole* man, even where, as in the Sermon on the Mount, the decalogue is pressed home to refer to "inward disposition." That a good "disposition" can take the place of the total goodness is quite unbiblical. The discovery of the so-called inner life dates from the Renaissance, probably from Petrarch. The "heart" in the biblical sense is not the inner life, but the whole man in relation to God. But as a man lives just as much from "outwards" to "inwards" as from "inwards" to "outwards," the view that his essential nature can be understood only from his intimate spiritual background is wholly erroneous.

I therefore want to start from the premise that God should not be smuggled into some last secret place, but that we should frankly recognize that the world, and people, have come of age, that we should not run man down in his worldliness, but confront him with God at

his strongest point, that we should give up all our clerical tricks, and not regard psychotherapy and existentialist philosophy as God's pioneers. The importunity of
all these people is far too unaristocratic for the Word
of God to ally itself with them. The Word of God is
far removed from this revolt of mistrust, this revolt
from below. On the contrary, it reigns.

Well, it's time to say something concrete about the
secular interpretation of biblical concepts; but it's too
hot!

If you want of your own accord to send[63] . . . extracts from my letters, you can, of course, do so. I
would not do it myself as yet, because you are the only
person with whom I venture to think aloud, as it were,
in the hope of clarifying my thoughts. But please yourself about it.

We shall very soon now have to be thinking a great
deal about our journey together in the summer of 1940,
and my last sermons.[64]

9 July. I must stop now. I think we shall meet again
soon.

16 July 1944

I heard yesterday that you had been moved again. I
hope to hear soon how you are getting on. The historic
atmosphere[65] sounds attractive, anyway. Only ten years
ago we should hardly have realized that the symbolic
crozier and ring, claimed by both emperor and pope,
could lead to an international political struggle. Weren't
they really *adiaphora*? We have had to learn again,
through our own experience, that they were not.

[63] "Albrecht Schönherr and others." A. S. later became a
Generalsuperintendent (Suffragan Bishop).

[64] A reference to East Prussia, where Hitler's headquarters
then were, and where the attempt on his life was shortly to be
made (20 July).

[65] Not far from Canossa.

Whether Henry IV's pilgrimage to Canossa was sincere or merely diplomatic, the picture of Henry IV in January 1077 has left its mark permanently on the thought of European peoples. It was more effective than the Concordat of Worms of 1122, which formally settled the matter on the same lines. We were taught at school that all these great disputes were a misfortune to Europe, whereas in point of fact they are the source of the intellectual freedom that has made Europe great.

There is not much to report about myself. I heard lately on the wireless (not for the first time) some scenes from Carl Orff's operas (and also *Carmina Burana*). I liked them very much; they were so fresh, clear, and bright. He has also produced an orchestral version of Monteverdi. Did you know that? I also heard a *concerto grosso* by Handel, and was again quite surprised by his ability to give such wide and immediate consolation in the slow movement, as in the *Largo*, in a way in which we wouldn't dare to any more. Handel seems to be more concerned than Bach with the effect of his music on the audience; that may be why he sometimes has a façade-like effect. Handel, unlike Bach, has a deliberate purpose behind his music. Do you agree?

I am very interested to read *The House of the Dead*,[66] and I am impressed by the non-moral sympathy that those outside have for its inhabitants. May not this amorality, the product of religiosity, be an essential trait of these people, and also help us to understand more recent events? For the rest, I am doing as much writing and composing as much poetry as my strength allows. I have probably told you before that I often get down to a bit of work[67] in the evening, as we used to. Of course, I find that pleasant and useful. That is all the news that I have about myself. . . . I

---

[66] By Dostoievsky.
[67] I.e. listening to foreign broadcasts.

am glad that K[laus] is in such good spirits; he was so depressed for some time.[68] I think all his worries will soon be over; I very much hope so for his own and his family's sake. . . .

If you have to preach in the near future, I should suggest taking some such text as Ps. 62.1; 119.94a; 42.5; Jer. 31.3; Isa. 41.10; 43.1; Matt. 28.20b; I should confine myself to a few simple but vital thoughts. One has to live for some time in a community to understand how Christ is "formed" in it (Gal. 4.19); and that is especially true of the kind of community that you would have. . . .

Now for a few more thoughts on our theme. I am only gradually working my way to the non-religious interpretation of biblical concepts; the job is too big for me to finish just yet.

On the historical side: There is one great development that leads to the world's autonomy. In theology one sees it first in Lord Herbert of Cherbury, who maintains that reason is sufficient for religious knowledge. In ethics it appears in Montaigne and Bodin with their substitution of rules of life for the commandments. In politics Machiavelli detaches politics from morality in general and founds the doctrine of "reasons of State." Later, and very differently from Machiavelli, but tending like him towards the autonomy of human society, comes Grotius, setting up his natural law as international law, which is valid *etsi deus non daretur*, "even if there were no God." The philosophers provide the finishing touches: on the one hand we have the deism of Descartes, who holds that the world is a mechanism, running by itself with no interference from God; and on the other hand the pantheism of Spinoza, who says that God is nature. In the last resort, Kant is a deist, and Fichte and Hegel are pantheists. Everywhere the

[68] A reference to the resistance movement.

thinking is directed towards the autonomy of man and the world.

(It seems that in the natural sciences the process begins with Nicolas of Cusa and Giordano Bruno and their "heretical" doctrine of the infinity of the universe. The classical *cosmos* was finite, like the created world of the Middle Ages. An infinite universe, however it may be conceived, is self-subsisting, *etsi deus non daretur*. It is true that modern physics is not as sure as it was about the infinity of the universe, but it has not gone back to the earlier conceptions of its finitude.)

God as a working hypothesis in morals, politics, or science, has been surmounted and abolished; and the same thing has happened in philosophy and religion (Feuerbach!). For the sake of intellectual honesty, that working hypothesis should be dropped, or as far as possible eliminated. A scientist or physician who sets out to edify is a hybrid.

Anxious souls will ask what room there is left for God now; and as they know of no answer to the question, they condemn the whole development that has brought them to such straits. I wrote to you before about the various emergency exits that have been contrived; and we ought to add to them the *salto mortale* (death-leap) back into the Middle Ages. But the principle of the Middle Ages is heteronomy in the form of clericalism; a return to that can only be a counsel of despair, and it would be at the cost of intellectual honesty. It is a dream that reminds one of the song *O wüsst ich doch den Weg zurück, den weiten Weg ins Kinderland.*[69] There is no such way—at any rate not if it means deliberately abandoning our mental integrity; the only way is that of Matt. 18.3, i.e. through repentance, through *ultimate* honesty.

[69] "Oh if only I knew the way back, the long way back to the land of childhood."

And we cannot be honest unless we recognize that we have to live in the world *etsi deus non daretur*. And this is just what we do recognize—before God! God himself compels us to recognize it. So our coming of age leads us to a true recognition of our situation before God. God would have us know that we must live as men who manage our lives without him. The God who is with us is the God who forsakes us (Mark 15.34). The God who lets us live in the world without the working hypothesis of God is the God before whom we stand continually. Before God and with God we live without God. God lets himself be pushed out of the world on to the cross. He is weak and powerless in the world, and that is precisely the way, the only way, in which he is with us and helps us. Matt. 8.17 makes it quite clear that Christ helps us, not by virtue of his omnipotence, but by virtue of his weakness and suffering.

Here is the decisive difference between Christianity and all religions. Man's religiosity makes him look in his distress to the power of God in the world: God is the *deus ex machina*. The Bible directs man to God's powerlessness and suffering; only the suffering God can help. To that extent we may say that the development towards the world's coming of age outlined above, which has done away with a false conception of God, opens up a way of seeing the God of the Bible, who wins power and space in the world by his weakness. This will probably be the starting-point for our "secular interpretation."

WHO AM I?

Who am I? They often tell me
I step from my cell's confinement
calmly, cheerfully, firmly,
like a squire from his country-house.
Who am I? They often tell me

I talk to my warders
freely and friendly and clearly,
as though it were mine to command.
Who am I? They also tell me
I bear the days of misfortune
equably, smilingly, proudly,
like one accustomed to win.

Am I then really all that which other men tell of?
Or am I only what I know of myself,
restless and longing and sick, like a bird in a cage,
struggling for breath, as though hands were compressing
    my throat,
yearning for colours, for flowers, for the voices of birds,
thirsting for words of kindness, for neighbourliness,
tossing in expectation of great events,
powerlessly trembling for friends at an infinite distance,
weary and empty at praying, at thinking, at making,
faint, and ready to say farewell to it all?
Who am I? This or the other?
Am I one person today, and tomorrow another?
Am I both at once? A hypocrite before others,
and before myself a contemptibly woebegone weakling?
Or is something within me still like a beaten army,
fleeing in disorder from victory already achieved?

Who am I? They mock me, these lonely questions of mine.
Whoever I am, thou knowest, O God, I am thine.

18 July 1944

I wonder whether any letters have been lost in the raids
on Munich. Did you get the one with the two poems?[70]
It was just sent off that evening, and it also contained
a few introductory remarks on our theological theme.
The poem about Christians and pagans contains an
idea that you will recognize: "Christians stand by God
in his hour of grieving"; that is what distinguishes
Christians from pagans. Jesus asked in Gethsemane,

[70] "Who am I?" and "Christians and Pagans."

"Could you not watch with me one hour?"[71] That is a reversal of what the religious man expects from God. Man is summoned to share in God's sufferings at the hands of a godless world.

He must therefore really live in the godless world, without attempting to gloss over or explain its ungodliness in some religious way or other. He must live a "secular" life, and thereby share in God's sufferings. He *may* live a "secular" life: i.e. he is freed (as one who has been liberated from false religious obligation inhibitions.) To be a Christian does not mean to be religious in a particular way, to make something of oneself (a sinner, a penitent, or a saint) on the basis of some method or other, but to be a man—not a type of man, but the man that Christ creates in us. It is not the religious act that makes the Christian, but participation in the sufferings of God in the secular life.

That is *metanoia*: not in the first place thinking about one's own needs, problems, sins, and fears, but allowing oneself to be caught up into the way of Jesus Christ, into the messianic event, thus fulfilling Isa. 53. Therefore "believe in the gospel,"[72] or, in the words of John the Baptist, "Behold, the Lamb of God, who takes away the sin of the world" (John 1.29). (By the way, Jeremias has recently asserted that the Aramaic word for "lamb" may also be translated "servant"; this is very appropriate in view of Isa. 53.)

This being caught up into the messianic suffering of God in Jesus Christ takes a variety of forms in the New Testament. It appears in the call to discipleship, in Jesus' table-fellowship with sinners, in "conversions" in the narrower sense of the word (e.g. Zacchaeus), in the act of the woman who was a sinner (Luke 7)— an act that she performed without any confession of

---

[71] Matt. 26.40.
[72] Mark 1.15.

sin, in the healing of the sick (Matt. 8.17; see above), in Jesus' acceptance of children. The shepherds, like the wise men from the East, stand at the crib, not as "converted sinners," but simply because they are drawn to the crib by the star just as they are. The centurion of Capernaum (who makes no confession of sin) is held up as a model of faith[73] (cf. Jairus).[74] Jesus "loved" the rich young man.[75] The eunuch (Acts 8) and Cornelius (Acts 10) are not standing at the edge of an abyss. Nathaniel is "an Israelite indeed, in whom there is no guile" (John 1.47). Finally, Joseph of Arimathea and the women at the tomb.[76] The only thing that is common to all these is their sharing in the suffering of God in Christ. That is their "faith."

There is nothing of religious method here. The "religious act" is always something partial; "faith" is something whole, involving the whole of one's life. Jesus calls men, not to a new religion, but to life. But what does this life look like, this participation in the powerlessness of God in the world? I will write about that next time, I hope.

Just one more point for today. When we speak of God in a "non-religious" way, we must speak of him in such a way that the godlessness of the world is not in some way concealed but for that very reason revealed rather in, and thus exposed to, an unexpected light. The world that has come of age is more godless, and perhaps its coming of age is nearer to God than before.

Forgive me for still putting it all so terribly clumsily and badly, as I really feel I am. . . . We are getting up at 1.30 almost every night here; it is a bad time, and it handicaps mental work.

[73] Matt. 8.
[74] Mark 5.
[75] Mark 10.
[76] Mark 15–16.

CHRISTIANS AND PAGANS

Men go to God when they are sore bestead,
Pray to him for succour, for his peace, for bread,
For mercy for them sick, sinning, or dead;
All men do so, Christian and unbelieving.

Men go to God when he is sore bestead,
Find him poor and scorned, without shelter or bread,
Whelmed under weight of the wicked, the weak, the dead;
Christians stand by God in his hour of grieving.

God goeth to every man when sore bestead,
Feedeth body and spirit with his bread;
For Christians, pagans alike he hangeth dead,
And both alike forgiving.

21 July 1944[77]

All I want to do today is to send you a short greeting.
I expect you are often with us here in your thoughts
and are always glad of any sign of life, even if the
theological discussion stops for a moment. These theological thoughts are, in fact, always occupying my
mind; but there are times when I am just content to
live the life of faith without worrying about its problems. At those times I simply take pleasure in the day's
Losungen[78]—in particular those of yesterday and today; and I am always glad to go back to Paul Gerhardt's beautiful hymns.

During the last year or so I have come to know and
understand more and more the profound this-worldliness of Christianity. The Christian is not a *homo religiosus*, but simply a man, as Jesus was a man—in
contrast, shall we say, to John the Baptist. I don't mean

[77] The day after the unsuccessful attempt to assassinate
Hitler.
[78] 20 July: Ps. 20.7; Rom. 8.31. 21 July: Ps. 23.1; John
10.24.

the shallow and banal this-worldliness of the enlight-
ened, the busy, the comfortable, or the lascivious, but
the profound this-worldliness, characterized by discipline and the constant knowledge of death and resurrection. I think Luther lived a this-worldly life in this
sense.

I remember a conversation that I had in A.[79] thir-
teen years ago with a young French pastor.[80] We were
asking ourselves quite simply what we wanted to do
with our lives. He said he would like to become a
saint (and I think it is quite likely that he did become
one). At the time I was very impressed, but I disagreed
with him, and said, in effect, that I should like to learn
to have faith. For a long time I did not realize the
depth of the contrast. I thought I could acquire faith
by trying to live a holy life, or something like it. I suppose I wrote *The Cost of Discipleship* as the end of
that path. Today I can see the dangers of that book,
though I still stand by what I wrote.

I discovered later, and I am still discovering right
up to this moment, that it is only by living completely
in this world that one learns to have faith. One must
completely abandon any attempt to make something
of oneself, whether it be a saint, or a converted sinner,
or a churchman (a so-called priestly type!), a righteous
man or an unrighteous one, a sick man or a healthy
one. By this-worldliness I mean living unreservedly in
life's duties, problems, successes and failures, experiences and perplexities. In so doing we throw ourselves
completely into the arms of God, taking seriously, not
our own sufferings, but those of God in the world—
watching with Christ in Gethsemane. That I think is
faith, that is *metanoia*; and that is how one becomes a
man and a Christian (cf. Jer. 45!). How can success

[79] America.
[80] Jean Lasserre.

make us arrogant, or failure lead us astray, when we share in God's sufferings through a life of this kind?

I think you see what I mean, even though I put it so briefly. I am glad to have been able to learn this, and I know I have been able to do so only along the road that I have travelled. So I am grateful for the past and present, and content with them. You may be surprised at such a personal letter; but if for once I want to say this kind of thing, whom should I say it to? May God in his mercy lead us through these times; but above all may he lead us to himself.

I was delighted to hear from you, and am glad you are not finding it too hot. There must be a good many letters from me on the way. Didn't we go more or less along that way in 1936?

Good-bye. Keep well, and don't lose hope that we shall all meet again soon.

STATIONS ON THE ROAD TO FREEDOM

Discipline

If you set out to seek freedom, then learn above all things
to govern your soul and your senses, for fear that your passions
and longings may lead you away from the path you should follow.
Chaste be your mind and your body, and both in subjection,
obediently, steadfastly seeking the aim set before them;
only through discipline may a man learn to be free.

Action

Daring to do what is right, not what fancy may tell you,
valiantly grasping occasions, not cravenly doubting—

freedom comes only through deeds, not through
thoughts taking wing.
Faint not nor fear, but go out to the storm and the
action,
trusting in God whose commandment you faithfully
follow;
freedom, exultant, will welcome your spirit with joy.

Suffering

A change has come indeed. Your hands, so strong
and active,
are bound in helplessness now you see your action
ended; you sigh in relief, your cause committing
to stronger hands; so you now may rest contented.
Only for one blissful moment could you draw near to
touch freedom;
then, that it might be perfected in glory, you gave it to
God.

Death

Come now, thou greatest of feasts on the journey to
freedom eternal;
death, cast aside all the burdensome chains, and
demolish
the walls of our temporal body, the walls of our souls
that are blinded,
so that at last we may see that which here remains
hidden.
Freedom, how long we have sought thee in discipline,
action, and suffering;
dying, we now may behold thee revealed in the Lord.

I wrote these lines in a few hours this evening. They
are quite unpolished, but they may perhaps please you
and be something of a birthday present for you.

I can see this morning that I shall again have to re-vise these lines completely. Still, I am sending them to you as they are, in the rough. I am certainly no poet!

25 July 1944

I like to write to you as often as I can now, because I think you are always glad to hear from me. There is nothing special to report about myself. . . . During the last few nights it has been our turn again round here. When the bombs come shrieking down, I always think how trivial it all is compared with what you are going through out there. It often makes me downright angry to see how some people behave in such situations, and how little they think of what is happening to other people. The danger here never lasts more than a few minutes. . . .

I have now finished Dostoievsky's *Memoirs from the House of the Dead*. It contains a great deal that is wise and good. I am still thinking about his assertion, which in his case is certainly not a mere conventional dictum, that man cannot live without hope, and that men who have really lost all hope often become wild and wicked. It may be an open question whether in this case hope = illusion. The importance of illusion to one's life should certainly not be underestimated; but for a Christian there must be hope based on a firm foundation. And if even illusion has so much power in people's lives that it can keep life moving, how great a power there is in a hope that is based on certainty, and how invincible a life with such a hope is. "Christ our hope"[81] —this Pauline formula is the strength of our lives.

They have just come to take me off to my exercise, but I will just finish this letter, to make sure that it goes today. I think of you every day. Your true and grateful friend. . . .

[81] I Tim. I.I.

27 July 1944

. . . It must be a relief to your mind that you have
plenty to do; at any rate, I should suppose so.

Your summary of our theological theme is very clear
and simple. The question how there can be a "natural
piety" is at the same time the question of "unconscious
Christianity," with which I am more and more concerned. Lutheran dogmatists distinguished between a
fides directa and a *fides reflexa*. They related this to the
so-called children's faith, at baptism. I wonder whether
this does not raise a far-reaching problem. I hope we
shall soon come back to it.

28 July 1944

. . . You think the Bible has not much to say about
health, fortune, vigour, etc. I have been thinking over
that again. It is certainly not true of the Old Testament.
The intermediate theological category between God and
human fortune is, as far as I can see, that of blessing.
In the Old Testament—e.g. among the patriarchs—
there is a concern, not for fortune, but for God's blessing, which includes in itself all earthly good. In that
blessing the whole of earthly life is claimed for God,
and it includes all his promises. It would be natural to
suppose that, as usual, the New Testament spiritualizes
the teaching of the Old Testament here, and therefore
to regard the Old Testament blessing as superseded in
the New. But is it an accident that sickness and death
are mentioned in connection with the misuse of the
Lord's Supper ("The cup of *blessing*," I Cor. 10.16;
11.30), that Jesus restored people's health, and that
while his disciples were with him they "lacked nothing?"[82] Now, is it right to set the Old Testament blessing against the cross? That is what Kierkegaard did.
That makes the cross, or at least suffering, an abstract

[82] Luke 22.35.

principle; and that is just what gives rise to an unhealthy methodism, which deprives suffering of its element of contingency on a divine ordinance. It is true that in the Old Testament the person who receives the blessing has to endure a great deal of suffering (e.g. Abraham, Isaac, Jacob, and Joseph), but this never leads to the idea that fortune and suffering, blessing and cross are mutually exclusive and contradictory—nor does it in the New Testament. Indeed, the only difference between the Old and New Testaments in this respect is that in the Old the blessing includes the cross, and in the New the cross includes the blessing.

To turn to a different point: not only action, but also suffering is a way to freedom. In suffering, the deliverance consists in our being allowed to put the matter out of our own hands into God's hands. In this sense death is the crowning of human freedom. Whether the human deed is a matter of faith or not depends on whether we understand our suffering as an extension of our action and a completion of freedom. I think that is very important and very comforting.

I am getting on all right, and there is nothing fresh to report about the family. Hans[83] is definitely down with diphtheria, but there seems to be good hope for him. Good-bye, and keep your spirits up as we are doing; and look forward, as we are doing, to meeting soon. *Neues Lied* No. 370.3–4.

MISCELLANEOUS THOUGHTS

Giordano Bruno: "There can be something frightening about the sight of a friend; no enemy can be so terrifying as he"—Can you understand that? I am trying hard, but I can't really understand it. Does "terrifying" refer to the inherent danger of betrayal, inseparable from close intimacy (Judas?)?

[83] Hans von Dohnanyi, who was also arrested on 5 April 1943.

Spinoza: Emotions are not expelled by reason, but only by stronger emotions.

❊ ❊ ❊

It is the nature, and the advantage, of strong people that they can bring out the crucial questions and form a clear opinion about them. The weak always have to decide between alternatives that are not their own.

❊ ❊ ❊

We are so constituted that we find perfection boring. Whether that has always been so I do not know. But I cannot otherwise explain why I care so little for Raphael or for Dante's *Paradiso.* Nor am I charmed by everlasting ice or everlasting blue sky. I should seek the "perfect" in the human, the living, and the earthly, and therefore not in the Apolline, the Dionysian, or the Faustian. In fact, I am all for the moderate, temperate climate.

❊ ❊ ❊

The beyond is not what is infinitely remote, but what is nearest at hand.

❊ ❊ ❊

Absolute seriousness is never without a dash of humour.

❊ ❊ ❊

The essence of chastity is not the suppression of lust, but the total orientation of one's life towards a goal. Without such a goal, chastity is bound to become ridiculous. Chastity is the *sine qua non* of lucidity and concentration.

❊ ❊ ❊

Death is the supreme festival on the road to freedom.

Please excuse these rather pretentious *"pensées."* They are fragments of conversations that have never taken place, and to that extent they belong to you. One who is forced, as I am, to live entirely in his thoughts, has the silliest things come into his mind—i.e. writing down his odd thoughts!

3 August 1944

. . . I wonder whether you will be moved again soon, and if so, where to. I should like to know whether you have read my poems. You must read the very long one (in rhyme), *Nächtliche Stimmen in Tegel*, some time later. I am enclosing the outline of a book that I have planned. I don't know whether you can get anything from it, but I think you more or less understand what I am driving at. I hope I shall be given the peace and strength to finish it. The Church must come out of its stagnation. We must move out again into the open air of intellectual discussion with the world, and risk saying controversial things, if we are to get down to the serious problems of life. I feel obliged to tackle these questions as one who, although a "modern" theologian, is still aware of the debt that he owes to liberal theology. There will not be many of the younger men in whom these two trends are combined. How very useful your help would be! But even if we are prevented from clarifying our minds by talking things over, we can still pray, and it is only in the spirit of prayer that any such work can be begun and carried through.

I have been reading about "tropical heat" in Italy. Is it very bad? . . . There is nothing to report about the family; I am always glad when I can write that. Goodbye.

OUTLINE FOR A BOOK

I should like to write a book of not more than 100 pages, divided into three chapters:

1. A Stocktaking of Christianity.
2. The Real Meaning of Christian Faith.
3. Conclusions.

Chapter 1 to deal with:

(*a*) The coming of age of mankind (as already indicated). The safeguarding of life against "accidents" and "blows of fate"; even if these cannot be eliminated, the danger can be reduced. Insurance (which, although it lives on "accidents," seeks to mitigate their effects) as a western phenomenon. The aim: to be independent of nature. Nature was formerly conquered by spiritual means, with us by technical organization of all kinds. Our immediate environment is not nature, as formerly, but organization. But with this protection from nature's menace there arises a new one—through organization itself.

But the spiritual force is lacking. The question is: What protects us against the menace of organization? Man is again thrown back on himself. He has managed to deal with everything, only not with himself. He can insure against everything, only not against man. In the last resort it all turns on man.

(*b*) The religionlessness of man who has come of age. "God" as a working hypothesis, as a stop-gap for our embarrassments, has become superfluous (as already indicated).

(*c*) The Protestant Church: Pietism as a last attempt to maintain evangelical Christianity as a religion; Lutheran orthodoxy, the attempt to rescue the Church as an institution for salvation; the Confessing Church: the theology of revelation; a δὸς μοὶ ποῦ στῶ[84] over against the world, involving a "factual" interest in Christianity; art and science searching for their origin. Generally in the Confessing Church: standing up for the Church's "cause," but little personal faith in Christ.

[84] See p. 132.

"Jesus" is disappearing from sight. Sociologically: no effect on the masses—interest confined to the upper and lower middle classes. A heavy incubus of difficult traditional ideas. The decisive factor: the Church on the defensive. No taking risks for others.

(d) Public morals—as shown by sexual behaviour.

Chapter 2.

(a) God and the secular.

(b) Who is God? Not in the first place an abstract belief in God, in his omnipotence etc. That is not a genuine experience of God, but a partial extension of the world. Encounter with Jesus Christ. The experience that a transformation of all human life is given in the fact that "Jesus is there only for others." His "being there for others" is the experience of transcendence. It is only this "being there for others," maintained till death, that is the ground of his omnipotence, omniscience, and omnipresence. Faith is participation in this being of Jesus (incarnation, cross, and resurrection). Our relation to God is not a "religious" relationship to the highest, most powerful, and best Being imaginable —that is not authentic transcendence—but our relation to God is a new life in "existence for others," through participation in the being of Jesus. The transcendental is not infinite and unattainable tasks, but the neighbour who is within reach in any given situation. God in human form—not, as in oriental religions, in animal form, monstrous, chaotic, remote, and terrifying, nor in the conceptual forms of the absolute, metaphysical, infinite, etc., nor yet in the Greek divine-human form of "man in himself," but "the man for others," and therefore the Crucified, the man who lives out of the transcendent.

(c) Interpretation of biblical concepts on this basis. (Creation, fall, atonement, repentance, faith, the new life, the last things.)

(*d*) Cultus. (Details to follow later, in particular on cultus and "religion.")

(*e*) What do we really believe? I mean, believe in such a way that we stake our lives on it? The problem of the Apostles' Creed? "What *must* I believe?" is the wrong question; antiquated controversies, especially those between the different sects; the Lutheran versus Reformed, and to some extent the Roman Catholic versus Protestant, are now unreal. They may at any time be revived with passion, but they no longer carry conviction. There is no proof of this, and we must simply take it that it is so. All that we can prove is that the faith of the Bible and Christianity does not stand or fall by these issues. Karl Barth and the Confessing Church have encouraged us to entrench ourselves persistently behind the "faith of the Church," and evade the honest question as to what we ourselves really believe. That is why the air is not quite fresh, even in the Confessing Church. To say that it is the Church's business, not mine, may be a clerical evasion, and outsiders always regard it as such. It is much the same with the dialectical assertion that I do not control my own faith, and that it is therefore not for me to say what my faith is. There may be a place for all these considerations, but they do not absolve us from the duty of being honest with ourselves. We cannot, like the Roman Catholics, simply identify ourselves with the Church. (This, incidentally, explains the popular opinion about Roman Catholics' insincerity.) Well then, what do we really believe? Answer: see (*b*), (*c*), and (*d*).

Chapter 3.
Conclusions:

The Church is the Church only when it exists for others. To make a start, it should give away all its property to those in need. The clergy must live solely on the free-will offerings of their congregations, or possibly engage in some secular calling. The Church must share in the secular problems of ordinary human life, not dominating, but helping and serving. It must tell men of every calling what it means to live in Christ, to exist for others. In particular, our own Church will have to take the field against the vices of *hubris*, power-worship, envy, and humbug, as the roots of all evil. It will have to speak of moderation, purity, trust, loyalty, constancy, patience, discipline, humility, contentment, and modesty. It must not underestimate the importance of human example (which has its origin in the humanity of Jesus and is so important in Paul's teaching); it is not abstract agrument, but example, that gives its word emphasis and power. (I hope to take up later this subject of "example" and its place in the New Testament; it is something that we have almost entirely forgotten). Further: the question of revising the creeds (the Apostles' Creed); revision of Christian apologetics; reform of the training for the ministry and the pattern of clerical life.

All this is very crude and condensed, but there are certain things that I am anxious to say simply and clearly—things that we so often like to shirk. Whether I shall succeed is another matter, especially if I cannot discuss it with you. I hope it may be of some help for the Church's future.

10 August 1944

. . . I can understand your no longer finding your memories "nourishing." But the strength of thankfulness continually gives strength to memories. It is in just such times that we should make an effort to remember in our prayers how much we have to be thankful for. Above all, we should never allow ourselves to be consumed by the present moment, but should foster that calmness that comes from noble thoughts, and measure everything by them. The fact that most people cannot do this is what makes it so difficult to bear with them. It is weakness rather than wickedness that perverts a man and drags him down, and it needs profound sympathy to put up with that. But all the time God still reigns in heaven.

I am now working on the three chapters that I wrote about. It is as you say: "knowing" is the most thrilling thing in the world, and that is why I am finding the work so fascinating.

14 August 1944

. . . There is hardly anything that can make one happier than to feel that one counts for something with other people. What matters here is not numbers, but intensity. In the long run, human relationships are the most important thing in life; the modern "efficient" man can do nothing to change this, nor can the demigods and lunatics who know nothing about human relationships. God uses us in his dealings with others. Everything else is very close to *hubris*. Of course, one can cultivate human relationships all too consciously in an attempt to mean something to other people, as I have been realizing lately in the letters of Gabriele von Bülow-Humboldt; it may lead to an unrealistic cult of the human. I mean, in contrast to that, that people are more important than anything else in life. That certainly does not mean undervaluing the world of things and practical efficiency. But what is the finest book, or picture, or house, or estate, to me, compared to my wife, my parents, or my friend? One can, of course, speak like that only if one has found others in one's life. For many today man is just a part of the world of things, because the experience of the human simply eludes them. We must be very glad that this experience has been amply bestowed on us in our lives. . . .

I have often noticed how much depends on what sort of demands we make on ourselves. Some people are spoilt by being satisfied with mediocrity, and so perhaps getting results more quickly; they have fewer hindrances to overcome. I have found it one of the most potent educative factors in our family that we had so many hindrances to overcome (in connection with relevance, clarity, naturalness, tact, simplicity, etc.) before we could express ourselves properly. I think you found it so with us at first. It often takes a long time to clear such hurdles, and one is apt to feel that one could have achieved success with greater ease and at less cost if these obstacles could have been avoided. . . .

God does not give us everything we want, but he does fulfil all his promises, i.e. he remains the Lord of the earth, he preserves his Church, constantly renewing our faith and not laying on us more than we can bear, gladdening us with his nearness and help, hearing our prayers, and leading us along the best and straightest paths to himself. By his faithfulness in doing this, God creates in us praise for himself.

21 August 1944

Once again I have taken up the *Losungen*[85] and meditated on them. The key to everything is the "in him." All that we may rightly expect from God, and ask him for, is to be found in Jesus Christ. The God of Jesus Christ has nothing to do with what God, as we imagine him, could do and ought to do. If we are to learn what God promises, and what he fulfils, we must persevere in quiet meditation on the life, sayings, deeds, sufferings, and death of Jesus. It is certain that we may always live close to God and in the light of his presence, and that such living is an entirely new life for us; that nothing is then impossible for us, because all things are possible with God; that no earthly power can touch us without his will, and that danger and distress can

[85] Num. 11.23; II Cor. 1.20.

only drive us closer to him. It is certain that we can claim nothing for ourselves, and may yet pray for everything; it is certain that our joy is hidden in suffering, and our life in death; it is certain that in all this we are in a fellowship that sustains us. In Jesus God has said Yes and Amen to it all, and that Yes and Amen is the firm ground on which we stand. In these turbulent times we repeatedly lose sight of what really makes life worth living. We think that, because this or that person is living, it makes sense for us to live too. But the truth is that if this earth was good enough for the man Jesus Christ, if such a man as Jesus lived, then, and only then, has life a meaning for us. If Jesus had not lived, then our life would be meaningless, in spite of all the other people whom we know and honour and love. Perhaps we now sometimes forget the meaning and purpose of our profession. But is not this the simplest way of putting it? The unbiblical idea of "meaning" is indeed only a translation of what the Bible calls "promise."

I feel how inadequate these words are to express my wish, namely to give you steadfastness and joy and certainty in your loneliness. This lonely birthday need not be a lost day, if it helps to determine more clearly the convictions on which you will base your life in time to come. I have often found it a great help to think in the evening of all those who I know are praying for me, children as well as grown-ups. I think I owe it to the prayers of others, both known and unknown, that I have often been kept in safety.

Another point: we are often told in the New Testament to "be strong" (I Cor. 16.13; Eph. 6.10; II Tim. 2.1; I John 2.14). Is not people's weakness (stupidity, lack of independence, forgetfulness, cowardice, vanity, corruptibility, temptability, etc.) a greater danger than evil? Christ not only makes people "good"; he makes them strong, too. The sins of weakness are the really

human sins, whereas the wilful sins are diabolical (and
no doubt "strong," too!). I must think about this again.
Good-bye; keep well, and don't lose confidence. . . .

23 August 1944

. . . Please don't ever get anxious or worried about me,
but don't forget to pray for me—I'm sure you don't!
I am so sure of God's guiding hand that I hope I shall
always be kept in that certainty. You must never doubt
that I am travelling with gratitude and cheerfulness
along the road where I am being led. My past life is
brim-full of God's goodness, and my sins are covered
by the forgiving love of Christ crucified. I am most
thankful for the people I have met, and I only hope
that they never have to grieve about me, but that they,
too, will always be certain of, and thankful for, God's
mercy and forgiveness. Forgive my writing this. Don't
let it grieve or upset you for a moment, but let it make
you happy. But I did want to say it for once, and I
could not think of anyone else who I could be sure
would take it aright.

Did you get the poem on freedom? It was very unpolished, but it is a subject about which I feel deeply.

I am now working at the chapter on "A Stocktaking
of Christianity." Unfortunately my output of work has
come to depend increasingly on smoking, but I am
lucky enough to have a good supply from the most
varied sources, so that I am getting on more or less.
Sometimes I am quite shocked at what I say, especially
in the first part, which is mainly critical; and so I am
looking forward to getting to the more constructive
part. But the whole thing has been so little discussed
that it often sounds too clumsy. In any case, it can't be
printed yet, and it will have to go through the "purifier"
later on. I find it hard work to have to write everything
by hand, and it seems hardly legible. (Amusingly
enough, I have to use German script, and then there

are the corrections!). We shall see; perhaps I shall write out a fair copy. . . .

I do so hope you will have a quiet time in body and mind. May God take care of you and all of us, and grant us the joy of meeting again soon. I am praying for you every day.

Your true and grateful friend,

D.

THE FRIEND

Not from the heavy soil,
where blood and sex and oath
rule in their hallowed might,
where earth itself,
guarding the primal consecrated order,
avenges wantonness and madness—
not from the heavy soil of earth,
but from the spirit's choice and free desire,
needing no oath or legal bond,
is friend bestowed on friend.

Beside the cornfield that sustains us,
tilled and cared for reverently by men
sweating as they labour at their task,
and, if need be, giving their life's blood—
beside the field that gives their daily bread
men also let the lovely cornflower thrive.
No one has planted, no one watered it;
it grows, defenceless and in freedom,
and in glad confidence of life untroubled
under the open sky.
Beside the staff of life,
taken and fashioned from the heavy earth,
beside our marriage, work, and war,
the free man, too, will live and grow towards the sun.
Not the ripe fruit alone—
blossom is lovely, too.
Does blossom only serve the fruit,
or does fruit only serve the blossom—

who knows?
But both are given to us.
Finest and rarest blossom,
at a happy moment springing
from the freedom of a lightsome, daring, trusting spirit,
is a friend to a friend.

Playmates at first
on the spirit's long journeys
to distant and wonderful realms
that, veiled by the morning sunlight,
glitter like gold;
when, in the midday heat
the gossamer clouds in the deep blue sky
drift slowly towards them—
realms that, when night stirs the senses,
lit by the lamps in the darkness,
like treasures prudently hidden
beckon the seeker.

When the spirit touches
man's heart and brow
with thoughts that are lofty, bold, serene,
so that with clear eyes he will face the world
as a free man may;
when then the spirit gives birth to action
by which alone we stand or fall;
when from the sane and resolute action
rises the work that gives a man's life
content and meaning—
then would that man,
lonely and actively working,
know of the spirit that grasps and befriends him,
like waters clear and refreshing
where the spirit is cleansed from the dust
and cooled from the heat that oppressed him,
steeling himself in the hour of fatigue—
like a fortress to which, from confusion and danger,
the spirit returns,
wherein he finds refuge and comfort and strengthening,
is a friend to a friend.

And the spirit will trust,
trust without limit.
Sickened by vermin
that feed, in the shade of the good,
on envy, greed, and suspicion,
by the snake-like hissing
of venomous tongues
that fear and hate and revile
the mystery of free thought
and upright heart,
the spirit would cast aside all deceit,
open his heart to the spirit he trusts,
and unite with him freely as one.
Ungrudging, he will support,
will thank and acknowledge him,
and from him draw happiness and strength.

But always to rigorous
judgment and censure
freely assenting,
man seeks, in his manhood,
not orders, not laws and peremptory dogmas,
but counsel from one who is earnest in goodness
and faithful in friendship,
making man free.

Distant or near,
in joy or in sorrow,
each in the other
sees his true helper
to brotherly freedom.

✻   ✻   ✻

At midnight came the air raid siren's song;
I thought of you in silence and for long—
how you are faring, how our lives once were,
and how I wish you home this coming year.

We wait till half past one, and hear at last
the signal that the danger now is past;
so danger—if the omen does not lie—
of every kind shall gently pass you by.

7

SIGNS OF LIFE

FROM THE PRINZ-ALBRECHT-STRASSE

28 December 1944

Dear Mother,

I AM SO GLAD to have just gotten permission to write you a birthday letter. I have to write in some haste, as the post is just going. All I really want to do is to help to cheer you a little in these days that you must be finding so bleak. Dear Mother, I want you to know that I am constantly thinking of you and Father every day, and that I thank God for all that you are to me and the whole family. I know you have always lived for us and have not lived a life of your own. That is why you are the only one with whom I can share all that I am going through. . . . Thank you for all the love that has come to me in my cell from you during the past year, and has made every day easier for me. I think these hard years have brought us closer together than we ever were before. My wish for you and Father . . . and for us all is that the New Year may bring us at least an occasional glimmer of light, and that we may once more have the joy of being together. May God keep you both well. With most loving wishes, dear, dear Mother, for a happy birthday.

Your grateful
Dietrich

POWERS OF GOOD

With every power for good to stay and guide me,
comforted and inspired beyond all fear,
I'll live these days with you in thought beside me,
and pass, with you, into the coming year.

The old year still torments our hearts, unhastening;
the long days of our sorrow still endure;
Father, grant to the souls thou hast been chastening
that thou hast promised, the healing and the cure.

Should it be ours to drain the cup of grieving
even to the dregs of pain, at thy command,
we will not falter, thankfully receiving
all that is given by thy loving hand.

But should it be thy will once more to release us
to life's enjoyment and its good sunshine,
that which we've learned from sorrow shall increase us,
and all our life be dedicate as thine.

Today, let candles shed their radiant greeting;
lo, on our darkness are they not thy light
leading us, haply, to our longed-for meeting?—
Thou canst illumine even our darkest night.

When now the silence deepens for our hearkening,
grant we may hear thy children's voices raise
from all the unseen world around us darkening
their universal paean, in thy praise.

While all the powers of good aid and attend us,
boldly we'll face the future, come what may.
At even and at morn God will befriend us,
and oh, most surely on each New Year's Day!

17 January 1945

Dear Parents,

. . . The last two years have taught me how little we
can get along with. . . . When we think how many

people every day now lose everything, we really have no right to call anything our own. . . .

Is H.W.[1] actually flying in the East now? And R[enate]'s husband? Thank you very much for your letter. . . . I read my letters here till I know them by heart.—Now for a few more requests: unfortunately there were no books handed in here for me today; Commissar Sonderegger would be willing to accept them every now and then. . . . I should be very grateful for them. There were no matches, face-cloths, or towel this time. Excuse my mentioning that; everything else was splendid. Could I please have some tooth-paste and a few coffee beans? Dear Father, could you get me from the library *Lienhard* and *Abendstunden eines Einsiedlers* by H. Pestalozzi, *Sozialpädagogik* by P. Natorp, and Plutarch's *Lives of Great Men*?

I am getting on all right. Do keep well. Many thanks for everything.

With fondest love,
Your grateful
Dietrich.

JONAH

In fear of death they cried aloud and, clinging fast
to wet ropes straining on the battered deck,
they gazed in stricken terror at the sea
that now, unchained in sudden fury, lashed the ship.
"O gods eternal, excellent, provoked to anger,
help us, or give a sign, that we may know
who has offended you by secret sin,
by breach of oath, or heedless blasphemy, or murder,

who brings us to disaster by misdeed still hidden,
to make a paltry profit for his pride."
Thus they besought. And Jonah said, "Behold,
I sinned before the Lord of hosts. My life is forfeit.

[1] Hans Walter Schleicher, Bonhoeffer's nephew.

Cast me away! My guilt must bear the wrath of God;
the righteous shall not perish with the sinner!"
They trembled. But with hands that knew no weakness
they cast the offender from their midst. The sea was there.
        (Written in Tegel prison in September 1944.)

THE PAST[2]

O happiness beloved, and pain beloved in heaviness,
you went from me.
What shall I call you? Anguish, life, blessedness,
part of myself, my heart—the past?
The door was slammed;
I hear your steps depart and slowly die away.
What now remains for me—torment, delight, desire?
This only do I know: that with you, all has gone.
But do you feel how I now grasp at you
and so clutch hold of you
that it must hurt you?
How I so rend you
that your blood gushes out,
simply to be sure that you are near me,
a life in earthly form, complete?
Do you divine my terrible desire
for my own suffering,
my eager wish to see my own blood flow,
only that all may not go under,
lost in the past?

Life, what have you done to me?
Why did you come? Why did you go?
Past, when you flee from me,
are you not still my past, my own?
As o'er the sea the sun sinks ever faster,
as if it moved towards the darkness,
so does your image sink and sink and sink
without a pause
into the ocean of the past,
and waves engulf it.

[2] After a visit from his fiancée.

As the warm breath dissolves
in the cool morning air,
so does your image vanish from me,
and I forget your face, your hands, your form.
There comes a smile, a glance, a greeting;
it fades, dissolves,
comfortless, distant,
is destroyed, is past.

I would inhale the fragrance of your being,
absorb it, stay with it,
as on hot summer days the heavy blossoms welcoming the
    bees
intoxicate them,
as privet makes the hawk-moths drunken—
but a harsh gust destroys both scent and blossoms,
and I stand like a fool
seeking a past that vanished.
It is as if parts of my flesh were torn out with red-hot
    pincers,
when you, a part of my life that is past, so quickly depart.
Raging defiance and anger beset me,
reckless and profitless questions I fling into space.
"Why, why, why?" I keep on repeating—
why cannot my senses hold you,
life now passing, now past?
Thus I will think, and think anew,
until I find what I have lost.
But I feel
that everything around me, over, under me
is smiling at me, unmoved, enigmatic,
smiling at my hopeless efforts
to grasp the wind,
to capture what has gone.

Evil comes into my eye and soul;
what I see, I hate;
I hate what moves me;
all that lives I hate, all that is lovely,
all that would recompense me for my loss.
I want my life; I claim my own life back again,

my past, yourself.
Yourself. A tear wells up and fills my eye;
can I, in mists of tears,
regain your image,
yourself entire?
But I will not weep;
only the strong are helped by tears,
weaklings they make ill.

Wearily I come to the evening;
welcome are bed and oblivion
now that my own is denied me.
Night, blot out what separates, give me oblivion,
in charity perform your kindly office;
to you I trust myself.
But night is wise and mighty,
wiser than I, and mightier than day.
What no earthly power can do,
what is denied to thoughts and senses, to defiance, to tears,
night brings me, in its bounty overflowing.
Unharmed by hostile time,
pure, free, and whole,
you are brought to me by dream,
you, my past, my life,
you, the day and hour but lately gone.

Close to you I waken in the dead of night,
and start with fear—
are you lost to me once more? Is it always vainly that I
    seek you,
you, my past?
I stretch my hands out,
and I pray—
and a new thing now I hear:
"The past will come to you once more,
and be your life's enduring part,
through thanks and repentance.
Feel in the past God's forgiveness and goodness,
pray him to keep you today and tomorrow."

8

THE LAST DAYS

(By Eberhard Bethge)

IT WAS LATE in the evening of Tuesday of Easter week, 3 April, 1945. The American artillery was rumbling in the west. An unwieldy closed vehicle, driven by gas generated by burning wood, drove out of the gates of Buchenwald into the night. Inside it the wood for the generator was piled up in the front. Behind it sixteen prisoners were trying to find room for themselves and the luggage that they still had in a space intended for eight people at the most. If one of them felt unwell, all his fellow-prisoners put their hands together, and he rested on them. There were Josef Müller, Captain Gehre, Generals von Falkenhausen and von Rabenau (with the latter Dietrich Bonhoeffer had shared a cell and played many games of chess during the last two months), Secretary of State Pünder, Wassili Kokorin (Molotov's nephew), airmen like the Englishman Hugh Falconer, Payne Best, von Petersdorff, and others—all the distinguished occupants of the windowless cellar in the Buchenwald camp. The truck stopped every hour, so that the pipes of the generator could be cleaned. There was no light inside, and nothing to eat and drink. Bonhoeffer found a tobacco ration among his treasures, and passed it round. By dawn the pile of wood had gone down, and the prisoners could take it in turns to stand, two at a time, by the little window in the door. Someone recognized a village. The direction in which they were travelling was not reassuring—it was clearly southeast. There was another camp there, and the men in the truck knew its name—Flossenbürg—and its purpose.[1] But the guards had even prepared a breakfast now.

On Wednesday of Easter week, a little before noon, they reached Weiden. Here it would have to be decided whether they would turn to the left into the narrow valley to Flossenbürg. They stopped; there was a brief conversation outside: "You must go on; we can't have you . . . too full." And the truck actually began to move again, straight on, to the south. Not to a death camp after all? But a few kilometres further on two mobile police signalled them to stop. A counter-order? Müller and Liedig, the captain of a frigate, were called out, and their luggage was taken out from the pile at the back. Dietrich Bonhoeffer leaned back, so as not to be seen. Gehre, the unlucky one with his black eyepatch, jumped out after them; he had shared a cell with Müller. (Josef Müller was to escape, but Gehre was to share Bonhoeffer's fate at Flossenbürg on 9 April.) At last they moved on again. There was now more room inside the truck, but the prisoners could not cast off their distress. But now, with Flossenbürg behind them, the guards were friendlier and more relaxed. They allowed the prisoners to alight at a farmhouse. Fresh air after so many months' imprisonment in a cellar! The men were allowed to use the pump in the yard, and a peasant woman brought a jug of milk and some rye bread. It was a lovely bright afternoon down the Nab valley.

At dusk the truck entered Regensburg. Here, too,

---

[1] It was an extermination camp.

there was overcrowding everywhere. At last a door was opened, and the men were ordered into the town prison. When they were treated too roughly, they protested. "Another lot of aristocrats," said a warder, "put them up on the second floor with the others." There in the corridors, lying or moving about, were the families of men like Goerdeler, Stauffenberg, Halder, and Hasselt, old and young, who had arrived earlier. The new arrivals had to go five into a single cell, but each of them chose his companions. Bonhoeffer was with von Rabenau, Pünder, von Falkenhausen, and Dr. Höppner, the brother of the general. The kitchens were already shut, but the prisoners made such a noise that at last one of the more timid warders produced some vegetable soup and distributed it, together with a slice of bread.

On that Thursday morning of Easter week, when the cell doors were opened so that the prisoners could wash, many of the prisoners recognized each other, and there were many introductions and exchanges of news. Best says that it was more like a great reception than a morning in prison. The warders tried in vain to make the men go back into their cells. At last, food was taken into the cells, and the "special cases" were again put behind bars. Bonhoeffer spent most of his time by the grille of his cell door, telling the various relatives what he knew about his fellow-prisoners in the Prinz-Albrecht-Strasse, where he had been kept till 7 February, and where, among other things, he had had many conversations with Böhm, Schlabrendorff, and Hans von Dohnanyi. He was able to tell Frau Goerdeler of the last weeks of her husband's life, and how he had been able to share with him the contents of the generous Christmas parcel that Commissar Sonderegger had accepted from Bonhoeffer's parents. Bonhoeffer was cheerful, and thought he was now out of the most dangerous area. Of course, no one could relieve or dispel his anxiety about his parents and his fiancée. An air raid warning interrupted the conversations, but when they came back from the cellar, the proceedings of the morning were repeated. Outside there was the railway shunting yard, a tangle of rails, engines, and carriages.

As the sun set, things grew quieter, and they were tired. But now one of the Buchenwald guards came back and took the men down to the familiar truck, and they drove out into the wet, windy night. They set off cheerfully along the Danube. But after a few kilometres the truck skidded and stopped. Falconer, the expert, confirmed that the steering-assembly was hopelessly broken. That could not be repaired on the road, and they had to trust to passers-by to ask the Regensburg police to send another truck. The guards were not very happy with their tommy-guns among the burnt-out cars on the open highway. The rain poured down more and more heavily as they waited.

In the morning light of Friday 6 April the guards at last allowed their charges to leave the truck so as to stretch their legs and warm themselves a little. At midday an uncommonly splendid bus with large unbroken windows arrived from Regensburg. The prisoners' belongings were put into it. Bonhoeffer still had with him a number of his beloved books: the Bible, Goethe, Plutarch. The Buchenwald guards, who had already become quite human, had to stay behind with the wreck, and ten new men of the S.S. Security Force, armed with tommy-guns, took over the transport. All the same, it was a new enjoyment to sit by the large windows and travel through the lovely countryside, up from the Danube, past the monastery at Metten into Stifter's Bavarian Forest. The village girls who asked for a lift were told by the driver that the people in his bus were a film company, going to make a propaganda film. The S.S. men fetched a capful of eggs from a farm, but only for themselves.

In the early afternoon they arrived at their destination: Schönberg below Zwiesel, a pretty village in the middle of the forest. At the village school they began to unload; the prisoners detained because of their family connections were already there. The group of "special cases" was taken to the first floor, into a light schoolroom with windows on three sides, overlooking the green valley. It contained real beds with coloured blankets. The door remained locked, but the weather was warm and sunny; Bonhoeffer sat for a long time at the open window and let the sun shine on him, chatted with Pünder, learnt Russian from Kokorin, and told him about the nature of Christian belief. They were all stimulated by their beautiful new surroundings; they laughed and ceremoniously wrote their names over their beds. Only the problem of food had not been solved. Complaints were answered with the explanation, which was certainly not incorrect, that the place was overcrowded with refugees from both east and west, and that no vehicle—nor, of course, petrol—was available for bringing food. To be sure, there were petrol and vehicles available later for other purposes. But finally the relatives who were detained, and who were freer, managed to make contact with sympathetic villagers, so that once they had a large dish of steaming potatoes, and the next day a potato salad.

Saturday was a good day for all of them. It began with a sensation: Best discovered an electric razor among his luggage, and all the men had the luxury of improving their feeling of well-being at the electric point. The conversation went from Moscow via Berlin to Lordon and back. The day was spent in language instruction, lying in the sun, and waiting for the unreal situation to have some kind of happy issue. The unusually large space made it possible to go for real walks. Everyone assumed that in the general confusion there could be no further judicial proceedings. In that place a firm bond united the members of enemy countries, without mistrust and with a great deal of humour.

But meantime the machinery was working methodically elsewhere, and was, in fact, able to put right relentlessly any merciful mistakes that had crept in.

In the afternoon of that Friday after Easter, the *SS Standartenführer* and *Regierungsdirektor* Walter Huppenkothen returned to Berlin from the concentration camp at Sachsenhausen. At a summary court-martial he and the camp commandant had just condemned to death Dohnanyi, Bonhoeffer's brother-in-law, who was lying half-conscious on a stretcher. On the previous day, after the daily meeting with Hitler, there had come into operation the whole plan determining which members of the resistance movement were to be executed, and which were to be transported further south. The next day Huppenkothen was again on his way south with petrol, much luggage, important files, and the diary of Admiral Canaris. He arrived at Flossenbürg concentration camp on the same day, and at once began to prepare for a summary court-martial. On 5 April Dr. Otto Thorbeck, the SS judge, was ordered to come from Nuremberg to preside at it. On the Sunday morning he travelled by goods train as far as Weiden, and toiled on a bicycle the remaining twenty kilometres up to Flossenbürg and his task. In the concentration camp itself there was a check to ensure that everything was ready for the final act to begin for Canaris, Oster, Sack, Strünk, Gehre, and Bonhoeffer. Bonhoeffer turned out to be missing. Where was he? During the night of Saturday to Sunday several cell doors were flung open and the occupants asked whether they were not Bonhoeffer who had been transferred from Buchenwald. "But *you* are Bonhoeffer" was twice shouted at Schlabrendorff, at Josef Müller, and at Liedig. So he was not there; he must have been held up on his way south. What did it matter? Transport and supplies of petrol were still func-

tioning in this organization, and there was still a whole
Sunday for the journey of almost 200 kilometres along
the hilly road to Schönberg and back.

In Schönberg Low Sunday was also celebrated in the
school building. It occurred to Pünder to ask Bonhoeffer to conduct a morning service. Bonhoeffer was
reluctant to do so, because most of his fellow-prisoners
were Roman Catholics. Besides, there was young
Kokorin, with whom Bonhoeffer had struck up a close
acquaintance—they had exchanged their Berlin and
Moscow addresses—and whom he probably did not
want to surprise into a religious service. But Kokorin
was in favour of the idea, and so Bonhoeffer yielded to
the general wish, and held a service. He read the *Qua-
simodo geniti* passage (I Peter 2.2ff.), prayed, and expounded to his comrades the text of the day: "and with
his stripes we are healed" (Isa. 53.5) and "Blessed be
the God and Father of our Lord Jesus Christ. By his
great mercy we have been born anew to a living hope
through the resurrection of Jesus Christ from the dead"
(I Peter 1.3). He spoke of the thoughts and decisions
that their eventful imprisonment together had brought
to them all. The prisoners detained for family reasons
had planned to smuggle Bonhoeffer into their room
after the service, so that they could have a service there
too. But it was not long before the door was flung
open, and two civilians called out: "Prisoner Bonhoeffer, get ready to come with us."

Bonhoeffer had time to get his things together. With
a blunt pencil he wrote in big letters his name and ad-
dress at the beginning, middle, and end of his Plutarch,
which he left there to provide some trace of himself in
the coming chaos. One of Goerdeler's sons kept the
book and gave it years afterwards—the last existing
sign of life—to the Bonhoeffer family. It was the last
book that Bonhoeffer had asked for in his last letter
from the Prinz-Albrecht-Strasse (17 January 1945),

and which he received for his birthday on 4 February, *via* Commissar Sonderegger.

He asked Payne Best to send special greetings to the Bishop of Chichester, if he succeeded in getting home again. "This is the end—for me the beginning of life" were the last words that Best hands down to us. Bonhoeffer hurried downstairs, taking with him Frau Goerdeler's final greeting.

The journey on that Sunday must have taken till the late evening. The members of the court-martial state that it met in full session. Thorbeck was the president, Huppenkothen counsel for the prosecution, and the camp commandant the assessor. They say that they cross-examined each one of the men and confronted them with each other: Canaris and Oster, Sack, the army judge who had at one time helped Perels so much in Berlin, Strünk and Gehre, and finally Dietrich Bonhoeffer. It was past midnight when Canaris returned to his cell after a prolonged absence. Knocking on the wall, he signalled to his neighbour, Colonel Lundig, a Dane, who has survived, that the end was near.

Before dawn, the first batch of those who were to join the mysterious convoy to the Alps left Flossenbürg; it included Schacht, Halder, von Bonin, the Schuschnigg family, and General Thomas. Gogalla, the commandant of the Prinz-Albrecht-Strasse prison, led the convoy, and had charge of the *Geheime Reichssache*, the document that contained the names of the prisoners who were to survive and have better treatment. On the way they stopped at Schönberg and fetched, among others, von Falkenhausen, Kokorin, Best, and Falconer. In Dachau Martin Niemöller was among those chosen.

In the grey dawn of that Monday, 9 April, there took place at Flossenbürg the execution of those who were not in any circumstances to survive. The camp doctor saw Bonhoeffer kneeling in the preparation cell and praying fervently. Later, Philipp of Hesse had in his cell a Bible and a volume of Goethe with Dietrich Bonhoeffer's name in them. On the same day Bonhoeffer's brother-in-law, Hans von Dohnanyi, was executed at Sachsenhausen.

> *Der die Sünde straft und gern vergibt,*
> *Gott, ich habe dieses Volk geliebt.*
> *Dass ich seine Schmach und Lasten trug*
> *und sein Heil geschaut—das ist genug.*
> *Halte, fasse mich! Mir sinkt der Stab,*
> *treuer Gott, bereite mir mein Grab.*[2]

[2] "God, who dost punish sin and willingly forgive, I have loved this people. That I have borne its shame and burdens, and seen its salvation—that is enough. Seize me and hold me! My staff is sinking; O faithful God, prepare my grave." (From *Der Tod des Mose*, written by Bonhoeffer in the late summer of 1944 [Lettner Verlag].)

GENERAL INDEX

INDEX OF BIBLICAL REFERENCES